Ins and Outs

of

Romanism

by

JOSEPH ZACCHELLO

LOIZEAUX BROTHERS
New York

Third Edition, 1956

Copyright 1949
by
Joseph Zacchello

Contents

Introduction

*No better friend than Christ—no better country
than the United States of America.*

The INS AND OUTS OF ROMANISM was written for fair-
minded readers who are deeply interested in the spiritual welfare of our country and its people. The interest of both will be
served best when Romanism is known as it is in fact—not as
told by over zealous Roman Catholics and uninformed non-
Catholics.

The greatest danger facing our country is the rising power
of the church of Rome, not only as a religious, but especially
as a political organization. We cannot remain indifferent to
this problem.

Millions of Roman Catholics in the United States are active
agents of the Pope. They are tireless in their zeal, and sincere
in their determination to make America Catholic by every possible means: the radio, the press, the movies, local and national
advertisement, personal and public work.

Their labor is not in vain, in fact, the religious world is
witnessing a remarkable paradox—an extraordinary decline of
Roman Catholicism in Roman Catholic countries, for instance
Italy, France, Spain, Brazil—but a conspicuous growth in some
of the countries traditionally Protestant, such as the United
States, England, Holland, Switzerland and the Scandinavian
countries.

Romanism is parading among non-Catholics like a victor-
ious army. Even those who do not join its ranks assume an
attitude of complacency, admiration, silence, apprehension and
even of fear.

We are going to take a look into the INS AND OUTS OF ROMANISM, not as a condemning judge, but as responsible citizens of this great country of ours in order to be enlightened, and thus be able to defend our Christian liberties as well as to protect ourselves, our families, our friends, and also Roman Catholics from the aims of Roman Catholicism.

New York City, November 1949   DR. JOSEPH ZACCHELLO

CHAPTER ONE

How The Pope Came Into Power

PART I

Steps in the Development of Papal Supremacy
(As outlined by historians)

We undertake to trace the story of the Roman see from the earliest evidence that can be found, to show that in the primitive times there neither existed in fact, nor was claimed as of right, any such supremacy as that which the see of Rome now claims; we undertake to show how the Roman power advanced step by step, in age after age, until at length, not by any prerogative divinely conferred on it from the beginning, but by a slow, gradual, and distinctly traceable progress, by means which, without forgetting the overruling control of the divine Providence, we may call simply natural, it attained its greatest fulness under such popes as Gregory VII in the latter half of the eleventh century, and Innocent III in the beginning of the thirteenth. ("Plain Lectures on the Growth of the Papal Power," James Craigie Robertson, M. A., pp. 4, 5. London: Society for Promoting Christian Knowledge.)

7

Out of the chaos of the great Northern migrations, and the ruins of the Roman Empire, there gradually arose a new order of states, whose central point was the papal see. Therefrom inevitably resulted a position not only new, but very different from the former. The new Christian Empire of the West was created and upheld by the Pope. The Pope became constantly more and more (by the state of affairs, with the will of the princes and of the people, and through the power of public opinion) the chief moderator at the head of the European common wealth, and, as such, he had to proclaim and defend the Christian law of nations, to settle international disputes, to mediate between princes and people, and to make peace between belligerent states. The Curia became a great spiritual and temporal tribunal. In short, the whole of Western Christendom formed, in a certain sense, a kingdom, at whose head stood the Pope and the emperor—the former, however, with continually increasing and far preponderating authority. ("The Church and the Churches," Dr. J. J. Ign. von Dollinger (R.C.), pp. 42, 43. London: Hurst and Blackett, 1862.)

IN THE SIXTH CENTURY.—The power of Rome seems to have made no further advance for some years after the middle of the sixth century. The Lombard wars and the plague depressed the energies of the Romans: and the see began to feel more sensibly the weight of Constantinopolitan influence when the conquests of Belisarius and Narses had brought Italy into subjection to the emperor of the East again. The patriarchs had never submitted to the popes; from Vigilius' time they were in open feud with Rome; and now they had often the authority of the emperor on their side against Rome. Vigilius was banished by Justinian. Pelagius I, who succeeded him, was opposed by the Romans, but supported by Narses, Justinian's general. ("The

Rise of the Papal Power," Robert Hussey, B. D., pp. 151, 152. Oxford: The Clarendon Press, 1863.)

DEGRADATION.—The immediate effect of the conquest of Italy (535-554) was the reduction of the popes to the degraded condition of the patriarchs of Constantinople. Such were the bitter fruits of their treason to the Gothic king. The success of Justinian's invasion was due to the clergy; in the ruin they brought upon their country, and the relentless tyranny they drew upon themselves, they had their reward. ("History of the Intellectual Development of Europe," John William Draper, M.D., LL.D., Vol. I, p. 355. New York: Harper & Brothers, copyright 1876.)

For above sixty years (883-955) the Roman Church was enslaved and degraded, while the apostolic see became the prey and the plaything of rival factions of the nobles, and for a long time of ambitious and profligate women. It was only renovated for a brief interval (997-1003) in the persons of Gregory V and Silvester II, by the influence of the Saxon emperor. Then the Papacy sank back into utter confusion and moral impotence; the Tuscan counts made it hereditary in their family; again and again dissolute boys, like John XII and Benedict IX, occupied and disgraced the apostolic throne, which was now bought and sold like a piece of merchandise, and at last three popes fought for the tiara, until the emperor Henry III put an end to the scandal by elevating a German bishop to the see of Rome. ("The Pope and the Council," Janus [Dr. J. J. Ign. von Dollinger, Roman Catholic] p. 100. London: Rivingtons, 1869.)

DEGENERACY IN THE TENTH CENTURY.—It is usual to denominate it the iron age, on account of its barbarism and barrenness of all good; also the leaden age, on account of the abounding wickedness by which it was deformed; and the dark age, on account of the scarcity of writers. . . . One can scarcely believe, nay, absolutely cannot credit, without ocular demonstration, what unworthy conduct, what base and enormous deeds, what execrable and abominable transactions, disgraced the Holy Catholic See, which is the pivot on which the whole Catholic Church revolves; when temporal princes, who, though called Christian, were most cruel tyrants, arrogated to themselves the election of the Roman pontiffs. Alas, the shame! Alas, the mischief! What monsters, horrible to behold, were then raised to the Holy See, which angels revere! What evils did they perpetrate; what horrible tragedies ensued! With what pollutions was this see, though itself without spot or wrinkle, then stained; what corruptions infected it; what filthiness defiled it; and hence what marks of perpetual infamy are visible upon it! ("Annales Ecclesiastic," C. Baronio, Roman Catholic [The Ecclesiastical Annals of Caesar Baronius, for the year 900], sects. 1, 3. Translation in Mosheim's History.)

DEGRADATION IN ELEVENTH CENTURY.— Throughout the greater part of the tenth and almost all the first half of the eleventh century, the Papacy had been sunk in the deepest moral degradation. This deplorable state of things had been created largely by the interference in the papal elections—which were nominally in the hands of the Roman clergy and people—by rival feudal factions at Rome which set up and pulled down popes at will. Through such influences it often happened that persons of scandalous life were, through violence and bribery, elevated to the papal chair. ("Mediaeval and Modern History," Philip Van Ness Myers, p. 113. Boston: Ginn & Co.)

ABSOLUTE AUTHORITY.—During this period [the thirteenth century] the organization of the papal hierarchy was perfected. At the head stood the all-powerful and absolute Pope as God's agent on earth; hence, at least in theory and claim, he was the ruler of the whole world in temporal and spiritual affairs. He was the defender of Christianity, the church, and the clergy in all respects. He was the supreme censor of morals in Christendom and the head of a great spiritual despotism. He was the source of all earthly justice and the final court of appeal in all cases. Any person, whether priest or layman, could appeal to him at any stage in the trial of a great many important cases. He was the supreme lawgiver of earth, hence he called all councils and confirmed or rejected their decrees. He might, if he so wished, set aside any law of the church no matter how ancient, so long as it was not strictly ordained by the Bible or by nature. He could also make exceptions to purely human laws, and these exceptions were known as dispensations. He had the sole authority to transfer or depose bishops and other church officers. He was the creator of cardinals and ecclesiastical honors of all kinds. He was the exclusive possessor of the universal right of absolution, dispensation, and canonization. He was the grantor of all church benefices. He was the superintendent of the whole financial system of the church and of all taxes. He had control over the whole force of the clergy in Christendom, because he conferred the *pallium*, the archbishop's badge of office. In his hands were kept the terrible thunders of the church to enforce obedience to papal law, namely, excommunication and the interdict.—"*The Rise of the Medioeval Church*," *Alexander Clarence Flick, Ph.D., Litt.D., pp.* 575, 576. *New York: G. P. Putnam's Sons,* 1909.

SCHISM—The schism arose from the struggle between two nations for the possession of the Papacy: the Italians wanted to regain and the French to keep it. And thus it came to pass that from 1378 to 1409 Western Christendom was divided into two, from 1409 to 1415, into three, Obediences. A Neapolitan, Urban

VI, had been elected, and his first slight attempt at a reform gave immediate occasion to the outbreak of the schism. Soon after entering on his pontificate, he excommunicated the cardinals who were guilty of simony. But simony had long been the daily bread of the Roman Curia and the breath of its life; without simony the machine must come to a standstill and instantly fall to pieces. The cardinals had, from their own point of view, ample ground for insisting on the impossibility of subsisting without it. They accordingly revolted from Urban and elected Clement VII, a man after their own heart. Nobody knew at the time whose election was the most regular, Urban's or Clement's. [p. 293] . . .

The situation was a painful one for all adherents of papal infallibility, who found themselves in an inextricable labyrinth. Their belief necessarily implied that the particular individual who is in sole possession of all truth, and bestows on the whole church the certainty of its faith, must be always and undoubtingly acknowledged as such. There can as little be any uncertainty allowed about the person of the right Pope as about the books of Scripture. Yet every one at that period must at bottom have been aware that the mere accident of what country he lived in determined which Pope he adhered to, and that all he knew of his Pope's legitimacy was that half Christendom rejected it. Spaniards and French men believed in Clement VII or Benedict XIII, Englishmen, and Italians in Urban VI or Boniface IX. What was still worse, the old notion, which for centuries had been fostered by the popes and often confirmed by them, of the invalidity of ordinations and sacraments administered outside the papal communion, still widely prevailed, especially in Italy. The papal secretary Coluccio Salutato paints in strong colors the universal uncertainty and anguish of conscience produced by the schism, and his own conclusion as a papalist is, that as all ecclesiastical jurisdiction is derived from the Pope, and as a Pope invalidly elected cannot give what he does not himself possess, no bishops or priests ordained since the death of Gregory XI could guarantee the validity of the sacraments they administered. It followed, according to him, that any one who adored the eucharist consecrated by a priest ordained in schism worshiped an idol. Such was the condition of Western Christendom. ("The Pope and the Council," Janus [Dr. J. J. Ign. von Dollinger, R. C.], pp. 293-296. London: Rivingtons, 1869.)

FALL.—With Boniface VIII fell the medieval Papacy. He had striven to develop the idea of the papal monarchy into a definite system. He had claimed for it the noble position of arbiter among the nations of Europe. Had he succeeded, the power which, according to the medieval theory of Christendom, was vested in the empire, would have passed over to the Papacy no longer as a theoretical right, but as an actual possession; and the Papacy would have asserted its supremacy over the rising state-system of Europe. His failure showed that with the destruction of the empire the Papacy had fallen likewise. Both continued to exist in name, and set forth their old pretensions; but the empire, in its old aspect of head of Christendom, had become a name of the past or a dream of the future since the failure of Frederick II. The failure of Boniface VIII showed that a like fate had overtaken the Papacy likewise. The suddenness and abruptness of the calamity which befell Boniface impressed this indelibly on the minds of men. The Papacy had first shown its power by a great dramatic act; its decline was manifested in the same way. The drama of Anagni is to be set against the drama of Canossa. ("A History of the Papacy," M. Creighton, D. D., Vol. I, p. 32. London: Longmans, Green & Co. 1899.)

CAPTIVITY.—That change of residence—the seventy years' residence of the popes at Avignon, France from 1305—marking as it does the time when the glories of the Papacy were over, and when it lost the political supremacy which it had previously enjoyed, has not inaptly been called the Babylonish captivity. It was the beginning of a new epoch in the history of the Papacy and the history of the empire—a period of decline for both. ("The See of Rome in the Middle Ages," Rev. Oswald J. Reichel, B. C. L., M. A., pp. 409, 410. London: Longmans, Green & Co., 1870.)

THE BORGIAS.—The next phase in which the Papacy exhibits itself is the natural result of the possession of absolute temporal and spiritual power; the next representative Pope is a Borgia. In no other place than Rome could a Borgia have arisen; in no other position than that of Pope could so frightful a monster have maintained his power. Alexander VI, or Roderic Borgia, a Spaniard of noble family and nephew to Pope Calixtus III, was early brought to Rome by his uncle, and made a cardinal in spite of his vices and his love of ease. He became Pope in 1492 by the grossest simony. Alexander's only object was the gratification of his own desires and the exaltation of his natural children. Of these, whom he called his nephews, there were five, one son being Caesar Borgia, and one daughter the infamous Lucrezia. Alexander is represented to have been a poisoner, a robber, a hypocrite, a treacherous friend. His children in all these traits of wickedness surpassed their father. Caesar Borgia, beautiful in person, and so strong that in a bull-fight he struck off the head of the animal at a single blow—a majestic monster ruled by unbridled passions and stained with blood—now governed Rome and his father by the terror of his crimes. Every night, in the streets of the city, were found the corpses of persons whom he had murdered either for their money or for revenge; yet no one dared to name the assassin. Those whom he could not reach by violence he took off by poison. His first victim was his own elder brother, Francis, Duke of Gandia, whom Alexander loved most of all his children, and whose rapid rise in wealth and station excited the hatred of the fearful Caesar. Francis had just been appointed duke of Benevento; and before he set out for Naples there was a family party of the Borgias one evening at the papal palace, where no doubt a strange kind of mirth and hilarity prevailed. The two brothers left together, and parted with a pleasant farewell, Caesar having meantime provided four assassins to waylay his victim that very night. The next morning the duke was missing; several days passed, but he did not return. It was believed that he was murdered; and Alexander, full of grief, ordered the Tiber to be dragged for the body of his favorite child. An enemy, he thought, had made away with him. He little suspected who that enemy was.

At length a Sclavonian waterman came to the palace with a startling story. He said that on the night when the prince disappeared, while he was watching some timber on the river, he saw two men approach the bank, and look cautiously around to see if they were observed. Seeing no one, they made a signal to two others, one of whom was on horseback, and who carried a dead body swung carelessly across his horse. He advanced to the river, flung the corpse far into the water, and then rode away. Upon being asked why he had not mentioned this before, the waterman replied that it was a common occurrence and that he had seen more than a hundred bodies thrown into the Tiber in a similar manner.

The search was now renewed, and the body of the ill-fated Francis was found pierced by nine mortal wounds. Alexander buried his son with great pomp, and offered large rewards for the discovery of his murderers. At last the terrible secret was revealed to him; he hid himself in his palace, refused food, and abandoned himself to grief. Here he was visited by the mother of his children, who still lived at Rome. What passed at their interview was never known; but all inquiry into the murder ceased, and Alexander was soon again immersed in his pleasures and his ambitious designs.

Caesar Borgia now ruled unrestrained, and preyed upon the Romans like some fabulous monster of Greek mythology. He would suffer no rival to live, and he made no secret of his murderous designs. His brother-in-law was stabbed by his orders on the steps of the palace. The wounded man was nursed by his wife and his sister, the latter preparing his food lest he might be carried off by poison, while the Pope set a guard around the house to protect his son-in-law from his son. Caesar laughed at these precautions. "What cannot be done in the noonday," he said, "may be brought about in the evening." He broke into the chamber of his brother-in-law, drove out the wife and sister, and had him strangled by the common executioner. He stabbed his father's favorite, Perotto, while he clung to his patron for protection, and the blood of the victim flowed over the face and robes of the Pope. Lucrezia Borgia rivaled, or surpassed, the crimes of her brother.

While Alexander himself performed the holy rites of the the church with singular exactness, in his leisure moments he poisoned wealthy cardinals and seized upon their estates. He is said to have been singularly engaging in his manners, and most agreeable in the society of those whom he had resolved to destroy. At length, Alexander perished by his own arts. He gave a grand entertainment, at which one or more wealthy cardinals were invited for the purpose of being poisoned, and Caesar Borgia was to provide the means. He sent several flasks of poisoned wine to the table, with strict orders not to use them except by his directions. Alexander came early to the banquet, heated with exercise, and called for some refreshment; the servants brought him the poisoned wine, supposing it to be of rare excellence; he drank of it freely, and was soon in the pangs of death. His blackened body was buried with all the pomp of the Roman ritual.

Scarcely is the story of the Borgias to be believed: such a father, such children have never been known before or since. Yet the accurate historians of Italy, and the careful Ranke, unite in the general outline of their crimes. On no other throne than the temporal empire of Rome has sat such a criminal as Alexander; in no other city than Rome could a Caesar Borgia have pursued his horrible career; in none other was a Lucrezia Borgia ever known. The Pope was the absolute master of the lives and fortunes of his subjects; he was also the absolute master of their souls; and the union of these two despotisms produced at Rome a form of human wickedness which romance has never imagined, and which history shudders to describe. ("Historical Studies," Eugene Lawrence, pp. 51-54. New York: Harper & Brothers, 1876.)

AT BEGINNING OF THE REFORMATION.—The downward course of the Papacy, from the time of Boniface VIII to the age of the Reformation, we have already contemplated. The removal of the papal see to Avignon, the Great Schism, the ever bolder demand for general councils which should be superior to the Pope, the history of these councils themselves and of what followed them, the internal moral corruption which in Innocent VIII and Alexander VI recalled the times of the pornocracy in the tenth century, from the pollution of which Hildebrand had saved the church, may be cited in illustration of the decline of which we speak. And yet at the beginning of the Reformation, the nimbus which surrounded the papal dignity had not disappeared, nor was that dignity the object of the first attack either of Luther or of Zwingli; only when Rome betrayed the trust reposed in her by the Reformers, and shut her ear to their cry for help, was this opposition regarded by them as a proof that instead of the Holy Father of Christendom they had to do with Antichrist. ("History of the Reformation in Germany and Switzerland Chiefly," Dr. K. R. Hagenback, Vol. I, p. 10. Edinburgh: T. & T. Clark, 1878.)

FUTURE EXTENSION.—It may be that the vicars of Jesus Christ have only begun their toil and their tutelage of the monarchies and dynasties of princes and their royal houses; that a wider, larger, and weightier mission is before them to the nations and confederation of commonwealths, and to the wayward turbulence of the popular will. The gospel of the kingdom has not yet assimilated to itself more than one third of the human race. The leaven is in the meal, but it has, as yet, penetrated only a portion. We know that "the whole must be leavened." The Christendom of today may be no more than the blade, or at most the stalk, to the full corn in the ear, which shall be hereafter. ("The Temporal Power of the Vicar of Jesus Christ," Henry Edward Manning, D. D., Roman Catholic, Preface, p. liii. London: Burns and Lambert, 1862.)

For more information about the Popes see "Source Book for Bible Students", copyrighted 1922, by Review and Herald Publishing Association, Washington, D. C.

PART II

Catholic and Scriptural Teachings about the Pope *

"We define that the Holy Apostolic See and the Roman Pontiff holds the primacy over the whole world, and the *Roman Pontiff himself is the successor of the Blessed Peter, prince of the Apostles, and the true vicar of Christ, the head of the whole church, the father of all Christians;* and that to him, in the person of Blessed Peter, was given, by Our Lord Jesus Christ, full power to feed, rule, and govern the universal church, as is' contained also in the acts of the ecumenical councils, and in the sacred canons." (COUNCIL OF TRENT)

"All names which in the Scriptures are applied to Christ, by virtue of which it is established that he is over the church, all the same names are applied to the pope." (BELLARMINE "ON THE AUTHORITY OF COUNCILS. VOL. 2. P. 266; ED. 1619)

"Hence he (the pope) is said to have a heavenly power, and hence *changes even the nature of things,* applying the substantial of one thing to another—*can make something out of nothing*—a judgment which is null he makes to be real, since in *the things which he wills, his will is taken for a reason.* Nor is there any one to say to him, Why dost thou do this? For he can dispense with the law, he can turn injustice into justice by correcting and changing the law, and he has the fullness of power. (DECRETALS OF GREGORY IX, BOOK 1, TITLE 7, CHAP. 3)

"Peter and his successor have power to impose laws both perceptive and prohibitive, power likewise to grant dispensation from these laws, and, when needful, to annul them. It is theirs

* Reprinted from my copyrighted pamphlet "The Pope."

to judge offenses against the laws, to improve and remit penalties. This judicial authority will even include the power to pardon sin. For sin is a breach of the laws of the supernatural kingdom, and falls under the cognizance of its constituted judges." (THE CATHOLIC ENCYCLOPEDIA, VOL. 12, P. 265)

"We hold upon this earth the place of God Almighty." (POPE LEO XIII IN THE ENCYCLICAL LETTER DATED JUNE 20, 1894)

"The pope is of such lofty and supreme dignity that, properly speaking, he has not been established in any rank of dignity, but rather *has been placed upon the very summit of all ranks of dignities.*

"Hence the pope is crowned with a triple crown, as king of heaven and of earth and of the lower regions.

"Moreover the superiority and the power of the Roman pontiff by no means pertains only to heavenly things, to earthly things, and to things under the earth, but are even over angels, than whom he is greater.

"So that if it were possible that the angels might err in the faith, or might think contrary to the faith, they could be judged and excommunicated by the pope.

"The pope is as it were God on earth, sole sovereign of the faithful of Christ, chief king of kings, having plenitude of power, to whom has been intrusted by the omnipotent God direction not only of the earthly but even of the heavenly kingdom.

"The pope is of so great authority that he can *modify,* explain, or interpret *even divine laws.* Whatever the Lord God Himself, and the Redeemer, is said to do, that His vicar does."

(*Extracts from Ferraris' Ecclesiastical Dictionary, article on the pope, published in Rome 1899 at the Press of the Propaganda*)

"For what is the subject in dispute when we discuss the primacy of the pontiff? In a few words, it is the sum and substance of Christianity. The inquiry is nothing less than, whether the church ought any longer to maintain its existence, or to be dissolved and to fall to ruin? What is the difference between asking whether it is expedient to remove the foundation from a building, the shepherd from his flock, the general from his army, the sun from the stars, the head from the body; and asking whether it is expedient that the building should fall, the flock be scattered, the army routed, the stars darkened, the body prostrate? (Bellarmine, "On the Chief Pontiff.")

"We have no right to ask reasons of the pope, any more than of Almighty God, as a preliminary to our submission. We are to take with unquestioning docility whatever instruction the pope gives us." ("The Catholic World," Aug. 1877.)

"Faithfully adhering to the tradition received from the beginning of the Christian faith, for the glory of God our Saviour, the exaltation of the Catholic Religion, and the salvation of Christian people, the Sacred Council approving we teach and define that it is a dogma divinely revealed that the Roman Pontiff, when he speaks ex-cathedra, that is, when in discharge of the office of pastor and teacher of all Christians, by virtue of his supreme Apostolic authority, he defines a doctrine regarding faith and morals to be held by the universal church, by the divine assistance promised him in the Blessed Peter, *is possessed of the infallibility* with which the Divine Redeemer willed that His Church should be endowed from defining doctrine regarding faith and morals; and that, therefore, *such definitions of the Roman Pontiffs are irreformable of themselves, and not from the consent of the church."* (VATICAN COUNCIL ON THE CHURCH OF CHRIST, CHAP. LV, JULY 18, 1870)

PARTS OF THE BULL OF BONIFACE VIII, "UNAM SANCTAM"

"We are compelled to believe with urgent faith and to hold one holy catholic and apostolic Church. Therefore, the one and only Church has one body and one head, not two heads like a monster, viz., Christ and the vicar of Christ, Peter and Peter's successor. We are instructed by the Gospels that there are in his power two swords, viz., the spiritual and the temporal. For when the apostles said 'Behold here are two swords' (Luke xxii. 38), viz., in the Church; when the apostles said so, the Lord did not respond, 'There are too many' but 'Enough.' Certainly, he who denies that there is in the power of Peter a temporal sword has paid poor attention to the word of the Lord, who said 'Put up the sword into the sheath' (John xviii. 11). Therefore, both are in the power of the Church, both the spiritual and the material sword. But this is to be wielded for the Church, that by the Church; that by the hand of the priest, this not by the hang of kings and soldiers, but at the nod and patience of the priest. Moreover, sword should be under sword, and the temporal authority should be subject to the spiritual; for when the apostle says 'There is no power except from God; the powers which be are ordained of God' (Rom. xiii. 1); they are not ordained except sword be under sword. For on the testimony of truth, the spiritual power has to institute the earthly, and to judge it, if it is not good. Thus, the prophecy of Jeremiah concerning the Church and the ecclesiastical power is verified, 'Behold, I have this day set thee over the nations and over the kingdoms,' etc. (Jer. i. 10). Therefore, if the earthly power deviates from the way, it shall be judged by the spiritual power; if the inferior spiritual power deviates, by its superior spiritual; but if the supreme by God alone, since it cannot be judged by man, on the testimony of the apostle, 'The spiritual man judgeth all things, but is himself judged of no man' (I Cor. ii. 15). Whoever, therefore, resists this power, thus ordained by God, resists the ordination of God; unless he feigns that there are two principles, like Manichaeus, which we judge false and heretical, because, on the testimony of Moses, God did not create the heavens and the earth in several principles but in one principle (Gen. i. 1). Then, to be subject to the Roman Pontiff, we declare, say, define, and pronounce to be absolutely necessary to every human creature to salvation."

SCRIPTURAL TEACHINGS ABOUT THE POPE

A—THE POPE IS NOT THE VICAR OF CHRIST

The pope is carried on men's shoulders.

Christ said: *"I am among you as he that serveth."* (LUKE 22:27)

The pope has men kiss his feet.
Christ washed men's feet. (JOHN 13:5)
The pope wears a triple crown of gold.
Christ wore a crown of thorns. (JOHN 19:5)
Christ's vicar on earth is the Holy Spirit and not a man. (JOHN 14 & 16)

How could an immoral man and an immoral writer such as pope Aeneas Sylvius be considered a vicar of Christ?

How could an immoral and wordly pope like Alexander VI (A.D. 1492-1503) be considered a vicar of Christ?

The most scholarly Roman Catholic historian of the popes, Ludwig Pastor, grants that Alexander lived the immoral life of the secular prince of his day, both as cardinal and as pope;

that he obtained the papacy by the rankest simony; and that he brought his high office into disrepute by his unconcealed nepotism and lack of moral sense." (HISTORY OF THE POPES, V;VI) His children, Caesar Borgia and Lucrezia, surpassed their father in wickedness.

Pope Innocent III (A.D. 1198-1216) ordered a crusade against the Christian Albigenses and demanded that they be put to death without mercy.

Did not Charles IX of France and his mother Catherine de Medicis, under orders from the pope, slaughter one hundred thousand Huguenots on *St. Bartholomew's Day,* Aug. 24, 1572?

Did not pope Pius V plot this crime with the French Court, and did not pope Gregory XIII sing the *"Te Deum"* for it in Rome?

Did not pope Innocent XI urge Louis XIV to revoke the *Edict of Nantes* (OCTOBER, 1685), and to persecute the French Huguenots?

The extirpation of the Albingenses, the massacre of the Waldenses, the martyrdoms of the Lollards, the slaughter of the Bohemians, the burning of Huss, Jerome, Savonarola, Frith, Tyndale, Ridley, Hooper, Cranmer, Latimer and thousands of others were ordered or approved by the so-called vicars of Christ, the popes.

The Roman Catholic Church teaches that no matter how evil a pope may be, he is still the vicar of Christ and his words and works are just as powerful.

But Scripture teaches that *"A corrupt tree cannot bring forth good fruit."* It is the inward nature which determines the outword actions. Therefore *"By their fruits ye shall know them."*

THE POPE IS NOT THE SUCCESSOR OF PETER

Peter would not accept homage of man. (ACTS 10:25, 26-REV. 22:8, 9)

The popes have not only accepted, but have demanded homage.

Peter did work miracles—such as raising the dead. (ACTS 9:40)

The popes do not claim the power of performing miracles.

Peter was inspired and had revealed truths which were not in the Old Testament.

The Roman Catholics do not claim that the pope is inspired.

If Peter was to have a successor with authority and power until the end of time why do not the Scriptures say *"submit to the pope,"* instead of saying *"Prove all things; hold fast that which is good."* (I THESS. 5:21)

"Beloved, believe not every spirit, but try the spirits whether they are of God; because many false prophets are gone out into the world." (I JOHN 4:17)

Were the humble, the spiritually-minded Apostle Peter to come to earth, would he recognize as his successor the proud Pontiff, who wears the triple crown; who is carried on the shoulders of the people and placed on the high altar of worship; who is called vicar of Christ; who is surrounded by foreign bayonets?

THE POPE IS NOT HEAD OF THE CHURCH OF CHRIST

Did not pope Gregory I (A.D. 590-604) repudiate the title of universal or ecumenical bishop? Was this not a plain denial of papal supremacy?

"St. Peter is not called Universal Apostle . . . the whole church falls from its place when he who is called Universal falls.

. . . But far from Christian hearts be that blasphemous name. . . . *I confidently affirm that who so calls himself, or desires to be called Universal Priest, in his pride goes before Antichrist."* (TO THE EMPEROR MAURICE, EPISTOLA 5:20-7:33)

The word pope is derived from the Greek *PAPAS*, Latin *PAPA*, meaning *"Father";* but Christ said: *"Call no man your father upon the earth; for one is your Father who is in heaven."* (MATT. 23:9). The bishop of Rome did not usurp the exclusive use of this title (pope) until the time of Hildebrand, pope Gregory VII (A.D. 1073-1085), before all bishops were called popes and in the Eastern branch of the church even the priests were called popes.

Christ is the only one who is referred to in the New Testament as the *head of the Church.* (EPH. 1:22, 23-5:23; COL. 1:18.) *Christ* is the only one in the New Testament called the *chief shepherd.* (JOHN 10:14; I PETER 5:4.) The only reference in the New Testament concerning a person who claims to have supreme power in the church on earth, is in connection with the prediction of the apostate church. (II THESS. 2:1; I TIM. 4:1-6)

THE POPE IS NOT INFALLIBLE

The Apostle warns the church of Rome, lest she should be *"cut off"* like the Jewish church, and perish; and exhorts her to be not *"high minded, but fear."* (ROM. 11:17, 22). How is this reconcilable with the doctrine of the infallibility of the pope?

How can a mere man be infallible? Is that not a prerogative of God alone?

"That man of sin shall be revealed, the son of perdition, who opposeth and exalteth himself above all that is called God, or that worshipped; so that he as God sitteth in the temple of God, showing himself that he is God." (II THESS. 2:3, 4)

How could pope Liberius (A.D. 352-366) be called infallible, when we know that he subscribed to an heretical Arian Creed, and broke communion with Athanasius, the great defender of the Nicene Creed?

Does not the condemnation of pope Honorius as a heretic by that Sixth General Council (IN A.D. 681), prove that the bishops of that time had no idea whatever of papal infallibility? *How can a pope be infallible and be condemned as a heretic?*

Were the popes infallible when they ordered Europe to exterminate the Moslems in the *medieval crusades*, promising heaven to all who died fighting the infidels?

How could one infallible pope, Eugenius IV (A.D. 1431-1447) condemn *Joan of Arc* (A.D. 1412-1431) to be burned alive as a witch, while another pope, Benedict XV, declares her a saint in 1919?

Were popes Paul V (A.D. 1605-1621) and Urban VIII (A.D. 1623-1644) infallible, when they condemned *Galileo* for holding a true scientific theory? *Did they not declare the Copernican theory was false, heretical, and contrary to the word of God?*

Did they not torture and imprison Galileo in the dungeons of the Inquisition for not sharing their erroneous views? In their decree prohibiting the book of Copernicus, "De Revolutionibus" the congregation of the index, March 5, 1619, denounced the new system of the mobility of the earth and the immobility of the sun as *"utterly contrary to the Holy Scriptures."*

If the Roman Catholics claim that the popes are infallible, how can they reconcile the contradictory decrees of Clement XIV *suppressing the Jesuits,* July 21, 1773, and pope Pius VII restoring them, Aug. 7, 1814?

"It was almost and indeed absolutely impossible for the church to enjoy a true and solid peace while this order (the Jesuits) existed." (POPE CLEMENT XIV IN HIS BRIEF "DOMINUS AC REDEMPTOR.")

Was pope Gregory XVI infallible when he condemned liberty of conscience, of opinion and of the press?

"From this polluted fountain of indifference flows that absurd and erroneous doctrine, or rather raving, in favor and defense of liberty of conscience, for which most pestilential error the course is opened to that entire and wild liberty of opinion . . . Hence that pest, of all others most to be dreaded in a state, unbridled liberty of opinion, licentiousness of speech, and a lust for novelty . . . Hither tends that worst and never sufficiently to

be execrated and detested liberty of the press." (ENCYCLICAL
LETTER DATED SEPT. 1832)

Is not the Roman teaching of infallibility opposed to the
freedom of thought? Is not a Roman Catholic hampered in
his search for the truth by a blind, degrading obedience to the
claims of an infallible pope?

The Roman Catholics claim that their church has and always
will teach the same doctrine. *Why do they need an infallible
pope if he has nothing new to teach?*

If the popes are infallible, why have popes contradicted each
other and been guilty of heresy?

A Council of Constantinople decreed that the image-worship
should be abolished; the Second Council of Nice declared against
the decree of Constantinople. The Council of Constance, Pisa,
and Basil declared that a Council was above a pope. The Council
of Florence and the Fifth Council of Lateran declared against
that doctrine.

There were two and even three rival popes at one time.
Who had then the privilege of infallibility to decide between
the claims of opposing popes?

"Give me leave to wonder," writes Chillingworth, *"That
St. Peter, the pretended bishop of Rome, writing two catholic
epistles, mentioning his departure, should not once acquaint the
Christians whom he writes to, what guide they were to follow
after he was taken from them: That the writers of the New
Testament should so frequently forewarn men of heretics, false
christs, false prophets, and not once arm them against them,
without letting them know this only sure means of avoiding their
danger: That so great part of the New Testament should be
employed about antichrist, and so little, or indeed none at all,
about the Vicar of Christ, and the guide of the faithful."* (REL.
PROT . . . LETTER TO LEWGAR. LONDON, 1845)

CHAPTER TWO

About Priests and Monks

The "PRIEST" among Roman Catholics is a sacred person, who offers sacrifices to God, and belongs to a sacred order or caste altogether distinct from, and officially superior to the laity, or common Christian people. The Council of Trent, whose doctrine and decrees must be believed by all Roman Catholics under pain of mortal sin and excommunication says:

"The priest is the man of God, the minister of God, the portion of God, the man called of God, consecrated to God, wholly occupied with the interests of God. He that despiseth him, despiseth God; he that hears him hears God. The priest remits sins as God, and that which he calls his body at the altar is adored as God by himself and by the congregation . . . It is clear that their (priests) function is such that none greater can be conceived wherefore they are justly called not only Angels, but also God, holding as they do among us the power and authority of the immortal God." (Catholic Doctrine as defined by the Council of Trent)

St. Alphonsus of Liguori, who is considered one of the leading doctors of Moral Theology, writes in his book, The Dignity and Duties of the Priest, or Selva:

"With regard to the power of priests over the real body of Christ, it is of faith that when they pronounce the words of consecration, the Incarnate God has obliged Himself to obey and to come into their hands under the sacramental appearance of bread and wine. We are struck with wonder when we find that in obedience to the words of His priests—Hoc est corpus meum—(This is my body), God Himself descends on the altar, that He comes whenever they call Him, and as often as they call Him, and places Himself in their hands, even though they should be their enemies. And after having come He remains, entirely at their disposal and they move Him as they please from one place to another. They may, if they wish, shut Him up in the tabernacle, or expose Him on the altar, or carry Him outside the Church; they may, if they choose, eat His flesh, and give Him for the food of others. Besides, the power of the priest surpasses that of the Blessed Virgin because she cannot absolve a Catholic from even the smallest sin.

Thus the priest may be called the creator of his Creator, since by saying the words of consecration he creates Jesus in the sacrament, by giving Him a sacramental existence, and produces Him as a victim to be offered to the eternal Father. As in creating the world it was sufficient for God to have said, Let it be made, and it was created—He spoke, and they were made—so it is sufficient for the priest to say "Hoc est corpus meum," and behold, the bread is no longer bread, but the body of Jesus Christ.

The power of the priest is the power of the divine person; for the transubstantiation of the bread requires as much power as the creation of the world. O the venerable sanctity of the hands! O happy function of the priest! He that created gave me the power to create Him; and He that created me without me is Himself created by me. As the word of God created heaven and earth so the words of the priest create Jesus Christ. When he ascended into heaven, Jesus Christ left his priests after Him to hold on earth His place of mediator between God and men, particularly on the altar."

According to the Bible teaching the one sacrifice which Christ offered to God for us when he died on the cross, is full, complete and no other sacrifice is needed (Heb. 9 and 10). All true Christians, as the Apostle Peter declares, constitute "a holy priesthood, to offer up spiritual sacrifices, acceptable to God by Jesus Christ" I Peter 2:5. (see also verse 9). The priests and ministers are only the religious teachers and guides of the people, not a separate cast or a holier class by the mere virtue of their office. We can go directly to Christ as our High Priest and one Mediator with God (I Tim. 2:5) without the ministry of another man, the priest. We can offer prayer and other spiritual sacrifices ourselves because we take the Lord Jesus Christ at His word as an all-sufficient Saviour. (Acts 4:12)

Before a man becomes a priest of the Roman Church, he receives six other orders. The 'Ordination' or 'The Sacrament of Orders' is the seventh one, and it is also one of the seven Sacraments. The Catechism of the Council of Trent says:

"*The tonsure* . . . is a sort of preparation for receiving orders. . . . In tonsure the hair of the head is cut in the form of a crown, and should be worn in that form, enlarging the crown according as the ecclesiastic advances in orders. This form of tonsure the Church teaches to be of apostolic origin. . . .

"*The order of porter* follows tonsure: its duty consists in taking care of the keys and door of the church, and suffering none to enter to whom entrance is prohibited. . . .

"The 2d among the Minor Orders is that of *reader*

[=lector], to him it belongs to read to the people, in a clear and distinct voice, the Sacred Scriptures, particularly the Nocturnal Psalmody; and on him also devolves the task of instructing the faithful in the rudiments of the faith. . . .

"The 3d order is that of *exorcist*: to him is given power to invoke the name of the Lord over persons possessed by unclean spirits. . . .

"The 4th and last among the Minor Orders is that of *acolyte*: the duty of the acolyte is to attend and serve those in Holy Orders, deacons and subdeacons, in the ministry of the altar. The acolyte also attends to the lights used at the celebration of the Holy Sacrifice, particularly whilst the Gospel is read. . . .

"Minor Orders . . . are, as it were, the vestibule through which we ascend to Holy Orders. Amongst the latter the 1st is that of *subdeacon*: . . . to him it belongs to prepare the altar-linen, the sacred vessels, the bread and wine necessary for the Holy Sacrifice, to minister water to the priest or bishop at the washing of the hands at mass, to read the epistle, a function which was formerly discharged by the deacon, to assist at mass in the capacity of a witness, and see that the priest be not disturbed by any one during its celebration. . . . At his consecration, . . . the bishop admonishes him that by his ordination he assumes the solemn obligation of perpetual continence. . . .

"The 2d amongst the Holy Orders is that of *deacon*: . . . to him it belongs constantly to accompany the bishop, to attend him when preaching, to assist him and the priest also during the celebration of the holy mysteries, and at the administration of the sacraments, and to read the gospel at the sacrifice of the mass. In the primitive ages of the church, he not unfrequently exhorted the faithful to attend to the divine worship, and administered the chalice in those churches in which the faithful received the holy eucharist under both kinds. In order to administer to the wants of the necessitous, to him was also committed the distribution of the goods of the church. To the deacons also, as the eye of the bishop, it belongs to inquire and ascertain who within his diocese lead lives of piety and edification, and who do not; who attend the holy sacrifice of the mass and the instructions of their pastors, and who do not; that thus the bishop, made acquainted by him with these matters, may be enabled to admonish each offender privately, or should he deem it more conducive to their reformation, to rebuke and correct them publicly. He also calls over the names of catechumens, and presents to the bishop those who are to be promoted to orders. In the absence of the bishop and priest, he is also authorized to expound the Gospel to the people, not however from an elevated place, to make it understood that this is not one of his ordinary functions. . . .

"The 3d and highest degree of all Holy Orders is the *Priesthood*. . . . The office of the priest is . . . to offer sacrifice to God, and to administer the sacraments of the church: the bishop, and after him the priests who may be present, impose hands on the candidate for priesthood; then placing a stole on his shoulders, he adjusts it in the form of a cross, to signify that the priest receives strength from above, to enable him to carry the cross of Jesus Christ, to bear the sweet yoke of his divine law, and to enforce this law, not by word only, but also by the eloquent example of a holy life. He next anoints his hands with sacred oil, reaches him a chalice containing wine and a paten with bread, saying: 'Receive power to offer sacrifice to God, and to celebrate mass as well for the living as for the dead.' By these words and ceremonies he is constituted an interpreter and mediator between God and man, the principal function of the priesthood. Finally, placing his hands on the head of the person to be ordained, the bishop says: 'Receive ye the Holy Ghost; whose sins you shall forgive, they are forgiven them: and whose sins you shall retain, they are retained'; thus investing him with that divine power of forgiving and retaining sins which was conferred by our Lord on his disciples. These are the principal and peculiar functions of the priesthood.

"The order of priesthood, although essentially one, has different degrees of dignity and power. The first is confined to those who are simply called priests, and whose functions we have now explained. The second is that of *bishops,* who are placed over their respective sees, to govern not only the other ministers of the church, but also the faithful; and, with sleepless vigilance and unwearied care, to watch over and promote their salvation.

. . . Bishops are also called 'pontiffs,' a name borrowed from the ancient Romans, and used to designate their chief priests. The third degree is that of *archbishop*: he presides over several bishops, and is also called 'metropolitan,' because he is placed over the metropolis of the province. Archbishops, therefore (although their ordination is the same), enjoy more ample power, and a more exalted station than bishops. *Patriarchs* hold the fourth place, and are, as the name implies, the first and supreme fathers in the episcopal order. Superior to all these is the sovereign pontiff, whom Cyril, archbishop of Alexandria, denominated in the council of Ephesus, 'the Father and Patriarch of the whole world.' . . .

"To the bishop belongs exclusively the administration of this sacrament. . . . Some abbots were occasionally permitted to confer Minor Orders: all, however, admit that even this is the proper office of the bishop, to whom, and to whom alone, it is lawful to confer the other orders: subdeacons, deacons, and priests are ordained by one bishop only, but . . . he himself is consecrated by three bishops."—from "The Catechism of the Council of Trent"—in any Roman Catholic book store.

There are two other main classes of Roman Priests: Secular or Diocesan Priests and Religious Priests. Secular or Diocesan Priests are those who are responsible only to the local Bishop or Cardinal. They make only the vow of chastity, not being required to make vows of poverty and obedience. Therefore they are allowed to own any kind of property except a wife. Disobedience to the Bishop does not put them in conflict with religion. These priests are usually in charge of parishes.

Religious Priests are those who belong to an order and make at least three vows (some of the Jesuits make four vows), viz., the vows of poverty, chastity, and obedience. Religious Priests are of two classes: Monks and plain Religious Priests. Both make the same three vows, but the vows of Monks are called *solemn vows* while those of the plain Religious Priests are called *simple vows*. Monks lose the right to possess even the least particle of private property, together with all personal rights and liberties. Plain Religious Priests cannot exercise the use of property, personal rights, or liberties; but they do not give up the fundamental right to possess them. For example: when a Monk dies, he has no property to leave to his relatives. Even if he inherits property he cannot accept it or pass it on when he dies. But when a plain Religious Priest dies, his relatives or those designated in his will, inherit his property; because he gave up only the use, not the ownership, while alive.

It is possible to belong to a religious order without being a priest by making vows either solemn or simple without ordination or consecration. Such as do this are called *brothers*.

But it is a little different with women. Those who make the

solemn vows are called Nuns, while those who take only the simple vows are called Sisters.

There is still another division among those who take simple vows. Some make simple vows for a limited period of time, usually three years. Others take perpetual vows. Some Sisters take only temporary vows, especially those who come in contact with the world; because this makes it easier for them to leave the sisterhood.

The place where Monks and Nuns live is called a Monastery, while the place where those who take simple vows live is called a Religious House.

When I was a priest I made a special study of priests, nuns, monks, sisters, etc. But very few Roman Catholics in America understand the differences that exist in the clergy. Even many priests are confused. In the United States the confusion is due to the fact that all members of the Roman clergy are called *Fathers,* when, ecclesiastically speaking, only Religious Priests should be called *Father*.

In Europe, where the clergy wear the habit of their order, even in public, it is easier for the people to distinguish the different kinds of priests and call them by their proper titles.

To enable you to better understand the difference between the Religious Priests and the Secular or Diocesan Priests, who usually serve in your community, I will give you a brief summary of the rules of the Benedictine System, which rules are followed by almost all monks and by many other religious orders. This is because Saint Benedict (480-543) is considered the founder of Monks in Europe. The main monastery of the Benedictine Fathers is Monte Cassino on the coast between Rome and Naples, Italy. It was founded in the year 529. You may secure a complete copy of the rules of the Benedictines in a large Catholic book store or by writing to St. Vincent's Abbey of Benedictine Order, Latrobe, Pennsylvania.

"According to the Rule of Benedict, the monks have to rise at 2 A.M. in the winter (and in summer, at such hours as the abbot directs); to the place of worship for vigils; and then spend the remainder of the night in committing psalms, private meditation, and reading. At sunrise they assemble for matins; then spend four hours in labor; then two hours in reading; then dine and read in private till 2:30 P.M., when they meet again for worship; and afterwards work till their vespers. In their vigils and matins 24 psalms are to be chanted each day, so as to complete the Psalter every week. Besides their social worship, seven hours each day are devoted to labor, two at least to private study, two to private meditation, and the rest to meals, sleep, and refreshment. The labor is agriculture, gardening, and various mechanical trades; and each one is put to such labor as his superior sees fit; for they all renounce wholly every species of personal liberty. They eat twice a day at a common table; first about noon, and then at evening. Both the quantity and the quality of their food are limited. To each is allowed one pound of bread per day, and a small quantity of wine. On the public table no meat is allowed, but always two kinds of porridge. To the sick, flesh is allowed. While at table, all conversation is prohibited; and some one reads aloud the whole time. They all serve as cooks and waiters by turns of a week each. Their clothing is simple, and regulated at the discretion of the abbot. Each is provided with two suits, a knife, a needle, and all other necessaries. They sleep in common dormitories of 10 or 20, in separate beds, without undressing, and have a light burning, and an inspector sleeping in each dormitory. They are allowed no conversation after they retire, nor at any time are they permitted to jest, or to talk for mere amusement. No one can receive a present of any kind, not even from a parent; nor have any correspondence with persons outside the monastery, except by its passing under the inspection of the abbot. A porter always sits at the gate, which is kept locked day and night; and no stranger is admitted without leave from the abbot; and no monk can go out, unless he has permission from the same source. The school for the children of the neighborhood is kept outside the walls. The whole establishment is under an abbot, whose power is absolute. His under officers are, a prior or deputy, a steward, a superintendent of the sick and the hospital, an attendant on visitors, a porter, etc., with the necessary assistants, and a number of deans or inspectors, who watch the monks at all times. The abbot is elected by the common suffrage of the brotherhood; and when in office, he appoints and removes his under officers at pleasure. On great emergencies, he summons the whole brotherhood to meet in council; and on more common occasions, only the seniors; but in either case, after hearing what each one is pleased to say, the decision rests wholly with himself. For admission to the society, a probation of 12 months is required; during which the applicant is fed and clothed, and employed in the meaner offices of the monks, and closely watched. At the end of his probation, if approved, he takes solemn and irrevocable vows of perfect chastity, absolute poverty, and implicit obedience to his superiors in every thing. If he has property, he must give it all away, either to his friends or the poor, or to the monastery; and never after must possess the least particle of private property, nor claim any personal rights or liberties. For lighter offenses, a reprimand is to be administered by some under officer. For greater offenses, after two admonitions, a person is deprived of his privileges, not allowed to read in his turn, or to sit at table, or enjoy his modicum of comforts. If still refractory, he is expelled from the monastery; yet still may be restored on repentance."

The Jesuits represent still another division in the Roman clergy. They are not monks, since they are without monastical life, i.e., they are not obliged to recite the canonical hours or divine office in the choir as monks must do for about four hours every day. They are not Secular or Diocesan Priests, even if they do dress like it, since they take three or four vows. They are not Religious Priests, since they take solemn vows rather than simple vows. They belong to a special category or separate class. A member of the Jesuits never became a pope, and never will, I believe, because there is a saying in Rome: "If you give the Keys of St. Peter to a Jesuit, he will never give them back.

"The operations of this powerful Society embrace every part of the world, and are carried on by means of the most intricate machinery ever devised by man. The Society is divided in five classes: 1st. Professed Members (Professi); 2nd. Spiritual Coadjutors; 3rd. Lay Coadjutors; 4th. Approved Pupils; 5th. The Novices.

"From his residence in Rome the General—or Black Pope—directs the movements of the Society in every part of the world by means of a system in which the art of investigation is brought to perfection. Every month or every quarter he receives reports from the heads of all the subordinate departments; and every third year the catalogues of every province, with detailed reports on the capacity and conduct of every member, are laid before him. Besides this, the most active correspondence is maintained with all parts of the world, in order to supply the offices of the Society with the information they require. In the central house at Rome are kept voluminous registers, in which are inscribed the names of all Jesuits, of their adherents, and of all the prominent persons, whether friends or enemies, with whom they have any connection. In these registers, it is said, are reported without alteration, without hatred, without passion, the facts relating to the life of each individual. It is the most gigantic biographical collection that has ever been formed. The frailties of a woman, the secret errors of a statesman, are chronicled in these books with the same cold impartiality. Drawn up for the purpose of being useful, these biographies are necessarily exact. When the Jesuits wish to influence an individual, they have but to turn to these volumes to know immediately his life, his character, his faults, his family, his friends, his most secret ties. By the use of such machinery the Order has attained its high position and widespread influence. (Harper's Weekly May 21, 1870.)

The Jesuits are the power behind the papal throne. To-day they are stronger in the United States than they ever were in any of the countries of Europe which expelled them as a menace to the government. They are still outlawed in many nations and also in several dioceses of Italy. The monks are generally known to be lazy, but the opposite is true of the Jesuits who, due to their unceasing activity, have gained considerable power.

CHAPTER THREE

Clerical Celibacy

Clerical Celibacy is not a precept of the divine or natural law, neither is it a dogma of the Roman Catholic Church. It is simply an obligatory law of the Western Roman Church which the pope can abolish any time he likes for all the priests or for some of them.—See Roman Catholic Question Box p. 311, Paulist Press, New York City.

The earliest law enforcing celibacy was passed by the Council of Elvira (Canon 33) in Spain about the year 300. Bishops, priests and deacons were to be deposed, if they lived with their wives and begot children after their ordination. A similar decree was enacted by a Roman Council under Pope Siricius (384-399), who wrote letters to Spain and Africa insisting upon its observance. A few years later Pope Innocent I (402-417) wrote similar letters to Bishops Victricius of Rouen and Exuperius of Toulouse. By the time of Leo the Great (440-461) the law of clerical celibacy was obligatory throughout the West.

The Eastern Churches followed a less strict line of development. The Council of Ancyra (Canon 10) in Galatia (314) permitted deacons to marry, if before their ordination they declared their intention of not leading a life of celibacy. The

Council of Neo-Caesarea (Canon 7) in Cappadocia (315) forbade priests to contract a new marriage under penalty of deposition. The Council of Nice (325) refrained from passing any law of celibacy (Socrates, *Hist. Eccles.*, i., 8), but forbade the clergy to have in their houses any woman who might excite suspicion about their morals; mothers, sisters and other relatives were excepted (Canon 3). The Apostolic Constitutions (400) forbade bishops, priests and deacons to marry after their ordination, but permitted them to keep their wives. The sixth canon indeed forbade bishops and priests to put away their wives "under pretext of piety."

The custom of insisting upon a celibate episcopate in the East (Ibid., v., 22) became a law under the Emperor Justinian (527-565). The custom also of allowing priests and deacons to live with the wives they had married before ordination became general about the middle of the seventh century, and was solemnly sanctioned by the Council of Trullo in 692.

This law with some slight modifications still holds good in the Eastern Churches to-day, whether uniate or schismatic. The Russian and Armenian schismatics, as a general rule, insists upon marriage as a condition of ordination to the secular priesthood, while their Bishops are chosen for the most part from the celibate monastic clergy. Second marriages are forbidden to priests. The Nestorians alone allow priests and deacons to marry after Ordination.

Leo X (1049-1054), St. Gregory VII (1073-1085), Urban II (1088-1099), and Calixtus II (1119-1124), made a determined fight against clerical concubinage, and the reform they inaugurated was permanent. The decree of the First Lateran Council (1123), which declared the marriage of all in sacred orders invalid was the official beginning of an official fight inside the church of Roman against celibacy.

Several centuries later it was necessary to make another and more authoritative law against married priests and the Council of Trent (1545) tried to settle the matter by its authoritative decision under pain of mortal sin and excommunication.

"The Council of Trent affirmed that those who had received merely the lower kinds of consecration, might marry on resigning their office, but a papal dispensation was necessary for all above a sub-deacon. A priest who marries incurs excommunication, and is debarred from all spiritual functions; and if a married man wants to become a priest he must leave his wife, who must of her own free will take the vow of chastity. In Session xxiv., Canon 9, the Council says, "Whoever shall affirm that persons in holy orders, or regulars, who have made a solemn profession of chastity, may contract marriage, and that the contract is valid, notwithstanding any ecclesiastical law or vow; and that to maintain the contrary is nothing less than to condemn marriage and that all persons may marry who feel, that though they should make a vow of chastity, they have not the will thereof; let him be accursed—for God does not deny His gifts to those who ask aright; neither does he suffer us to be tempted above that we are able. Canon 10: Whoever shall affirm that the conjugal state is to be preferred to a life of virginity or celibacy, and that it is not better and more conducive to happiness to remain in virginity or celibacy, than to be married; let him be accursed."

The Churches of the Reformation restored the liberty of marriage to the clergy. In their address to the Diet at Augsburg, 1530, the Reformers say:

"There has been general complaint among persons of every

rank, on account of the scandalous licentiousness and lawless lives of the priests; who were guilty of lewdness, and whose excesses had risen to the highest pitch. In order to put an end to such odious conduct, to adultery, and other lewd practices, several of our ministers have entered the matrimonial state. They themselves declare, that in taking this step they were influenced by the dictates of conscience, and a sacred regard for the holy volume, which expressly informs us, that marriage was appointed of God to prevent licentiousness: as Paul says (I Cor. vii. 2), 'To avoid fornication, let every man have his own wife.' Again, 'It is better to marry than to burn,' (I Cor. vii. 9); and according to the declaration of Christ, that not all men can receive this word. (Matt. xix. 12.) In this passage, Christ himself, who well knew what was in man, declares that few persons are qualified to live in celibacy; for 'God created us, male and female.' (Gen. i. 27.) And experience has abundantly proved how vain is the attempt to alter the nature, or meliorate the character, of God's creatures by mere human purposes or vows, without a peculiar gift or grace of God. It is notorious that the effort has been prejudicial to purity of morals; and in how many cases it has occasioned distress of mind, and the most terrific apprehensions of conscience, is known by the confessions of numerous individuals. Since, then, the word and law of God cannot be altered by human vows or enactments, the priests for this and other reasons have entered into the conjugal state. It is moreover evident from the testimony of history and the writings of the Fathers, that it was customary in former ages for priests and deacons to be married. Hence the injunction of Paul to Timothy (I Tim. iii. 2); 'A bishop then must be blameless, *the husband of one wife.*' It is but four hundred years since the clergy in Germany were compelled by force to abandon the matrimonial life, and submit to a vow of celibacy; and so generally and resolutely did they resist this tyranny, that the Archbishop of

Mayence, who published this papal edict, was well nigh losing his life in a commotion excited by the measure. And in so precipitate and arbitrary a manner was that decree executed, that the pope not only prohibited all future marriage of the priests, but even cruelly rent asunder the social ties of those who had long been living in the bonds of lawful wedlock, thus violating alike not only the laws of God, and the natural and civil rights of the citizen, but even the canons which the popes themselves made, and the decrees of the most celebrated Councils.—If therefore, it is evident from the divine word and command, that matrimony is lawful in ministers, and history teaches that their practice formerly was conformed to this precept; if it is evident that the vow of celibacy has been productive of the most scandalous and unchristian conduct of adultery, unheard of licentiousness, and other abominable crimes, among the clergy, as some of the dignitaries at Rome, have themselves often confessed and lamented, it is a lamentable thing that the Christian estate of matrimony has not only been presumptuously forbidden, but in some places speedy punishment has been inflicted, as though it were a heinous crime! Matrimony is moreover declared a lawful and honorable estate, by the laws of your imperial majesty, and by the code of every empire in which justice and law prevailed. Of late, however, innocent subjects, and especially ministers, are cruelly tormented on account of their marriage. Nor is such conduct a violation of the divine laws alone, it is equally opposed to the canons of the Church. The apostle Paul denominates that a doctrine of devils which forbids marriage (I Tim. iv. 1-3)."

The Emperor Charles V. favored a relaxation of the law, and so did some of the bishops; but in vain—Rome prevailed—and the yoke remains on the necks of the clergy to this day.

"The Thirty-second Article of the Church of England, and

the Twenty-first of the Methodist Confession, being a revision of the former, teach that it is lawful for ministers as well as other Christians, to marry at their own discretion. They "are not commanded by God's law, either to vow the estate of single life, or to abstain from marriage."

There is no such command in Scripture; there is no example of such vow—but abundance of testimony to the contrary. Yet Roman officials dare to appeal to the Scripture for support.

Rev. Thos. O. Summers, S.T.D., LL.D. in "*Errors of The Roman Catholic Church*" by James H. Chambers, St. Louis, Missouri, writes:

"Any one can see plainly enough why the Pope and the hierarchy of Rome are so strenuous in enforcing the celibacy of the clergy, and of monks and nuns, and why they so hate and denounce Luther, Cranmer, and other Reformers, for breaking the accursed bonds, and proclaiming their freedom. The Pope and his prelates want to have absolute control of the priestly and monastic orders, and so they doom them to a life of celibacy, that they might be made more available as ecclesiastical janizaries—available for all places and all occasions throughout their spiritual empire. They are bound by no domestic ties, restrained to no locality, ready at a moment's notice to go whithersoever their services are needed. Illicit connections can be formed and dissolved *ad libitum*. This, indeed, gives amazing power to the hierarchy, and wonderfully subserves all its projects and intents; and that is the reason why the oft-repeated and passionate request of the clergy, to be allowed to marry, to save themselves from a life of misery in contending against nature, or doing worse, yielding to its demands by living in debauchery, has been, still is, and is likely to be, persistently and emphatically refused.

We conclude this discussion by a passage from Jeremy Taylor's curious, learned, and masterly dissertation, "Of the Marriage of Bishops and Priests." (Works, vol. III., page 579.) Speaking of the law requiring celibacy, the erudite and eloquent prelate says:

'The law of the Church was an evil law, made by an authority violent and usurped, insufficient as to that charge; it was not a law of God—it was against the rights and against the necessities of nature; it was unnatural and unreasonable; it was not for edification of the Church; it was no advantage to spiritual life: it is a law, therefore, that is against public honesty, because it did openly and secretly introduce dishonesty [unchastity]; it had nothing of the requisites of a good law; it had no consideration of human frailty, nor of human comforts; it was neither necessary, nor profitable, nor innocent—neither fitted to time, nor place, nor person; it was not accepted by them that could not bear it; it was complained of by them that could; it was never admitted in the East; it was fought against and declaimed and railed at in the West; and at last, is laid aside in the Churches especially of the North, as the most intolerable and most unreasonable tyranny in the world; for it was not to be endured, that upon the pretence of an unreasonable perfection, so much impurity should be brought into the Church, and so many souls thrust down to hell.' "—Rev. Thos. O. Summer.

It is my contention that no Christian church has the right to bar from the ministry those who marry. The word of God does not exclude ministers when it says: "Increase and multiply" (Gen. 1:23); "To avoid fornication, let every man have his own wife" (I Cor. 7:2); "It is better to marry than to burn" (I Cor. 7:9); ". . . doctrines of devils . . . forbidding marriage" (I Tim. 4:3).

The Roman Church is responsible for the evil committed by those who "burn" and are not allowed to marry. I do not know how many nuns, priests, bishops, cardinals, and popes really keep the letter and the spirit of the vow of chastity; but it is amazing to read what the great Saints of the Roman Church had to do in order to keep themselves pure. And who among our modern Roman Catholic clergy is following the example of the Saints?

The seraphic Francis, the father of the Franciscans, who lived in the thirteenth century, though devoted to chastity, and brimful of the spirit, was, it seems, sometimes troubled with the movements of the flesh. An enemy that wrought within was difficult to keep in subjection. His saintship, on these occasions, adopted an effectual way of cooling this internal flame, and allaying the carnal conflict. He stood in winter to the neck in a pit full of icy water. One day, being attacked in an extraordinary manner by the demon of sensuality, he stripped naked, and belabored his importunate back with a disciplinarian whip; and then, leaving his cell, he buried his body, naked as he was, in a deep wreath of snow. The cold bath, the knotted thong, and the snowy bed were necessary for discharging the superabundant caloric of his saintship's constitution.

Godric, an English hermit, was troubled with the same complaint, and had recourse to the same remedy. He was a native of Norfolk, had visited Jerusalem, wept over the sacred sepulchre, and kissed, in holy devotion, the tomb of Emmanuel and the monument of redemption. He lived on the banks of the Werus, and was the companion of the bear and the scorpion, which were gentle and obliging to the man of God. But he had to contend, even in his solitude, with temptation. Satan, assuming the form of a lion or a wolf, endeavored to allure him from his duty. These outward trials, however, were nothing compared with the inward conflicts arising from the ferment of concupiscence and "the lusts of the flesh." He counteracted the rebellion of his blood, however, by the rigor of discipline. The cold earth was his only bed; and a stone, which he placed under his head, was his nightly pillow. The herb of the field and the water of the spring were his meat and drink, which he used only when compelled by the assaults of hunger and thirst. Clothed in haircloth, he spent his days in tears and fasting. The hermit, with these applications in keeping the body under, used a sufficiently cooling regimen. During the wintry frost and snow, he immersed himself in the stream of Werus, where, pouring forth prayers and tears, he offered himself a living victim to God. The flesh, it is likely, after this nightly dip, was discharged of all unnecessary heat, and became duly cool. But the Devil, it seems, played some pranks on the hermit, while he was enjoying the cold bath, and freezing his body for the good of his soul. Satan sometimes ran away with Godric's clothes, which were on the banks. But Godric terrified Beelzebub with shouts, so that, affrighted, he dropped his haircloth garment and fled.

Ulric's history is of a similar kind. He was born near Bristol, and fought the enemies of the human race for twenty years. He was visited, notwithstanding, with the demon of licentiousness. He fought the demon by the cold bath, and fasted till his skin was the only remaining covering of his bones. He nightly descended into a vessel filled with freezing water, and during the hours of darkness continued, in this comfortable place, which constituted his headquarters, to sing the Psalms of David.

Thomas Aquinas, the Angelic Doctor, required angelic aid to counteract the natural disposition of the mind, or rather of the flesh. He was born of a noble family, and enjoyed the benefit of a Parisian education. His friends opposed, but in vain, his resolution of immuring himself in the monastical retreats. He resisted their attempts with signal success, though it seems not always with spiritual weapons. He chased one woman, who opposed his resolution, with a firebrand. "The blessed youth," says the Roman Breviary, 'praying on bended knees before the cross, was seized with sleep, and seemed, through a dream, to undergo a constriction of a certain part by angels, and lost from that time forward all sense of concupiscence." His angelic saint-ship's natural propensity required supernatural power to restrain its fury. The grasp of angels was necessary to allay his carnality, and confer continence.

Benedict, in his necessity, had recourse to a pointed remedy. This saint, like Aquinas, was born of a noble family. He was educated at Rome, and devoted himself wholly to religion or rather to superstition. He lived three years in a deep cave, and in his retreat wrought many miracles. He knocked the Devil out of one monk with a blow of his fist, and out of another with the lash of his whip. But Satan, actuated by malice, and envious of human happiness, appeared to Benedict in the form of a blackbird, and renewed in his heart the image of a woman whom he had seen at Rome. The Devil in this matter rekindled the torch of passion, and excited such a conflagration in the flesh, that the saint nearly yielded to the temptation. But he soon, according to Mabillon, discovered a remedy. Having un-dressed himself, he rolled his naked body on nettles and thorns, till the lacerated body through pain lost all sense of pleasure. The father of the Benedictines, it appears, had his own difficulty in attempting to allay the ferment of the flesh.

What is happening to those priests and monks who do not believe in jumping "during winter in a pit full of icy water," at St. Francis did? or rolling naked "on nettles and thorns," as

St. Benedict did? or who are not receiving the ministry of angels to relieve their carnality, as St. Thomas Aquinas did?

The Roman Catholic clergy in the United States can use the privilege of a "Secret Marriage," since our liberal government guarantees such against the interference of Roman Catholic officials. I suggest this remedy to those who are afraid of a public papal excommunication, and prefer a union legalized by the laws of our country to other stratagems.

CHAPTER FOUR

Official Information on Romanism

PART I

Church Government

The material contained in this chapter was taken from an official Roman Catholic pamphlet: the *Vest Pocket Book of Catholic Facts* by the Most Reverend John Francis Noll, D.D., LL.D., Bishop of Fort Wayne, Indiana and founder of the National Roman Catholic weekly, *Our Sunday Visitor;* tenth and revised edition—90,000 printed by Our Sunday Press, Huntington, Indiana. Not copyrighted.

Council of the Pope—The Council of the Pope is the Sacred College of Cardinals, which, since 1586, consists of seventy members, who are divided as follows: Six Cardinal-Bishops, fifty Cardinal-priests, and fourteen Cardinal-deacons. There are always several vacancies, however.

The duties of most Cardinals in Rome consist in aiding the Pope in the discharge of ecclesiastical affairs. Outside of Italy the Cardinalate is often conferred to honor a country or a diocese, as well as to recognize worth.

The Sacred Congregations—In the government of the Church throughout the world the Pope is assisted greatly by Congregations of Cardinals, divided as follows: 1. Congregation of the Holy Office: 2. The Consistorial Congregation; 3. The Congregation of the Sacraments; 4. The Congregation of the Council; 5. The Congregation of the Religious; 6. The Congregation of the Propagation of the Faith; 7. The Congregation of Rites; 8. The Congregation of Ceremonies; 9. The Congregation for extraordinary Ecclesiastical Affairs; 10. The Congregation of Studies; 11 The Congregation for the Oriental Church. Space prevents the outlining of the special objects of all these Congregations. The Congregation of the Holy Office is to maintain the purity of religious faith, and therefore considers matters relating to heresy, the abuse of the Sacraments, etc. The Consistorial Congregation considers the names proposed for Bishoprics, erects new dioceses, and deals with matters relating to such affairs.

Tribunals of the Roman Curia—1. The Sacred Penitentiary. There are certain serious crimes and sins reserved for absolution to the Holy See. This Tribunal considers these cases in addition to requests for dispensations relating to the revalidation of marriages, etc. It is composed of the Cardinal Penitentiary and his several assistants.

2. The Sacred Rota. This Tribunal is composed of ten prelates appointed by the Pope. These are divided into groups who discharge their office in rotation, hence the name. It meets twice a week and considers ecclesiastical causes referred to it from any part of the world.

The territory of the world is divided into dioceses over which bishops or (in places sparsely settled by Catholics) vicars-apostolic are placed by the Holy See. These in turn are subdivided into parishes, over which priests rule spiritually as pastors in the name of the Church.

3. Supreme Tribunal of the Apostolic Signature. This Tribunal considers petitions which do not require judicial procedure, but depend upon the good will of the Holy Father. Frequently favors sought may imply prejudice to another party, when weighed carefully before being presented to His Holiness. Its officers meet twice a month.

The Offices of the Curia

1. The Apostolic Chancery. This Tribunal sends out letters of the Holy See, except those which are sent under the seal of the "Fisherman." It employs many clerks and its officers meet tri-weekly.

2. The Apostolic Datary. This Tribunal explains and dispatches favors granted by the Pope. It confers benefices, considers dispensations from ecclesiastical impediments to marriages, from vows, etc. This court meets daily and its recommendations receive the approbation and signature of the Pope.

3. The Apostolic Chamber. This Tribunal has charge of matters relating to finances and meets twice a week.

4. The Secretariate of State. This Tribunal deals with such political affairs as must be considered at the Vatican.

5. The Secretariate of Briefs. This Tribunal expedites letters which are given in the form of Briefs, and to which the seal of the "Fisherman" is attached.

ECUMENICAL COUNCILS. A General or Ecumenical Council is one convoked by the head of the Church and attended by Bishops from all parts of the world. There have been twenty of them, not including the Council of Jerusalem held by the Apostles. They were as follows:

1. At Nice (A.D. 325) at which the heresy of Arius was condemned and the Nicene Creed drafted.

2. At Constantinople (A.D. 381) which condemned the Macedonians and amplified the Nicene Creed, defining the divinity of the Holy Ghost.

3. At Ephesus (A.D. 431) which declared against Nestorius that Mary deserves to be called the Mother of God, defining that there is only one Person in Christ.

4. At Chalcedon (A.D. 451) which condemned the teaching of Eutyches, which held that there is only one nature in Christ.

5. At Constantinople (A.D. 553) which dealt again with Nestorianism and other heresies.

6. At Constantinople (A.D. 680) which condemned the teaching that there is only one will in Christ. In Christ's perfect human nature there must be a human will.

7. At Nice (A.D. 787). It condemned the Iconoclasts.

8. At Constantinople (A.D. 869). It condemned the errors of Photius, Greek Patriarch and the new schism he created, backed by the Emperor of Constantinople.

9. At the Lateran, Rome (A.D. 1123) which determined the rights of the Church in the election of Bishops, etc.

10. At the Lateran, Rome (A.D. 1139). It condemned the

errors of the Albigenses and decided matters relating to the Sacraments.

11. At the Lateran, Rome (A.D. 1179) which condemned the Waldenses and prescribed the mode of electing the Pope and Bishops.

12. At the Lateran, Rome (A.D. 1215). Disciplinary matters were drafted, including the obligation of annual Confession and Communion.

13. At Lyons, France (A.D. 1245). The Emperor Frederick II was excommunicated at this Council.

14. At Lyons, France (A.D. 1274). Its purpose was to unite the Roman and Greek Church; it did so only temporarily.

15. At Vienne, France (A.D. 1311). Here the Order of Knights Templars was condemned along with certain errors.

16. At Constance (A.D. 1414): Here it was decided which of three claimants was the true Pope, and the errors of Wickliffe were condemned.

17. At Florence (A.D. 1439). This Council declared the supremacy of the Pope over the whole Church and many Schismatic Bishops of the East submitted.

18. At the Lateran, Rome (A.D. 1512-1517). Decrees of the Schismatic Councils of Basle and Pisa were condemned and certain reforms promulgated.

19. At Trent (A.D. 1545-1563). This dealt with Lutheranism and promulgated the ancient Catholic teaching with reference to matters controverted. Reform measures were drafted. The Catechism of the Council of Trent is one result.

20. At the Vatican, Rome (A.D. 1869, suspended to the present date). The doctrine of papal infallibility was defined and modern infidelity condemned.

The Parish Church—In many Protestant denominations the parish unit is a distinct entity, the congregation issuing a call to the minister it would like to have serve it. In the Catholic Church the territory of the world is divided into dioceses with a Bishop at the head, who, in turn, parcels out the territory into parishes, over which he appoints pastors. Therefore, the parish units are like the branch postoffices in every city, town and hamlet in the United States, which have a close connection with Washington, and act as the Government's agents locally. They may also be likened to the branches of the National Bank distributed over the country. Washington appoints postmasters, prescribes the conditions upon which even their deputies may hold positions. Therefore, when we deal with the local postoffice, we are dealing with the United States Government. It receives our letters and carries them to any part of the world for us and brings to us correspondence from any country of the globe.

So the Church brings us in touch with the ordinances of Christ, and with the divine blessings of religion in our own locality.

For order's sake, definite territory is assigned to parishes in the cities. Those within any defined radius must go to their particular parish church for baptisms, marriages, Easter duty. The erection of the parochial buildings as well as their support becomes the obligation of the people who patronize them.

Most congregations have a parish school, because the Church has not only been commissioned to teach, but, as God's loyal agent, may not permit her children to grow up without such definite religious instruction as is needed for the building of a definite religious life.

The Catholic parish serves the people in a spiritual way from the time they enter into the world until they die, and even after their death those who were members of the parish are remembered frequently at the altar. Every Sunday the pastor offers his Mass for parishioners living and dead. The parish church is in use, not only on Sunday, but every day, and its doors are open from morning to night for people to visit their Saviour in His Eucharistic presence.

Religious Orders of Women

We have referred to the Franciscan and Dominican Nuns in connection with our brief treatises on the institutions of St. Francis and St. Dominic. Some Religious Sisterhoods are engaged exclusively in school work; others exclusively in hospital work; some do both; others devote themselves to the care of the aged, the orphan, the poor.

The largest Order of teaching nuns in the United States is that of the School Sisters of Notre Dame, who have nearly five thousand members in the Province of Baltimore, Milwaukee, Winona, and St. Louis. Another large Community which devotes itself entirely to school teaching in grammar, high schools, and colleges is that of the Sisters of Providence, with headquarters at St. Mary-of-the-Woods, Vigo County, Indiana. Still another is the Order of Ursulines, with establishments in many dioceses.

The Sisters of the Holy Cross, with headquarters at Notre Dame, Indiana, have charge of schools all over the country, though they also conduct some hospitals. This is true of several branches of the Franciscan Sisters also. The Sisters of Notre

Dame of Namur have charge of Trinity College, Washington, D. C.

The Sisters of Mercy, the Sisters of Charity of St. Vincent de Paul, and other branches of the same name, are occupied principally with hospital work.

The Sisters of the Good Shepherd devote themselves mainly to the care of delinquent girls, orphans and foundlings.

Then there are Contemplative Orders, such as the Carmelites, Poor Clares, the Visitation Nuns who are strictly cloistered.

Some Sisterhoods have the whole United States as their Province; others are divided among two or more Provinces; and still others, such as the Sisters of St. Joseph and Sisters of Mercy, are separate entities in the different dioceses.

In all there are more than 50,000 Sisters who are devoted to the spiritual and corporal works of mercy in the United States.

Then there are several organizations of a semi-religious character, who engage in social service work in our cities or who labor among the neglected Catholic poor. Notable among the latter is the Society of Missionary Catechists, with headquarters at Huntington, Indiana, whose special work is among the Spanish-Americans and Mexicans in the United States. They instruct adults in their own home, the children before or after school hours, and serve clothing and medicine to the needy.

The Servants of the Most Blessed Trinity, with headquarters at Cottonton, Alabama, do much the same work as the Missionary Catechists, but their work is not restricted to any particular field. At present they have schools in Puerto Rico. In addition to these there are the Mission Helpers, Servants of the Sacred Heart, whose Motherhouse is located at Towson, Maryland.

Religious Orders for Men

Benedictines—Founded by St. Benedict, who died in the year 543. The Church owes much to this Order which gave her 28 popes, more than 200 Cardinals, 1600 Archbishops, 4,000 Bishops and 16,000 Abbots.

There are several communities of Benedictine nuns, whose rule is modeled after that of St. Benedict.

Franciscans—The Friars Minor were founded by St. Francis of Assisi in 1209. They have had charge of the sacred places in the Holy Land for 700 years. They wear a brown garb, consisting of tunic and cowl, with a cincture of wool. About one hundred of their number are honored as Saints.

Distinct bodies comprise the Friars Minor, though all observe the rule of St. Francis. The Friars Minor proper were founded in 1209; the Conventuals in 1517; the Capuchins in 1528 and the Friars Minor of the Leonine Union in 1896.

St. Francis also founded the Poor Clares, who are known as the Second Order, they have eight monasteries in the United States.

Various Brotherhoods and Sisterhoods, who are engaged in teaching and nursing, belong to the Third Order Regular. There are five branches of the Brothers and thirty-three of the Sisters.

Francis also founded the Third Order for lay people—the Third Order, Secular.

The Capuchins number nearly twelve hundred in the Foreign Missions. In the United States they are divided between the Province of St. Joseph, with headquarters at Detroit, and the Province of St. Augustine, at Pittsburgh.

Dominicans—St. Dominic was a contemporary of St. Francis of Assisi, and founded the "Order of Preachers" in 1216. The original purpose of the Order was to combat heresy by preaching. We owe the Rosary in its present form to St. Dominic. The Dominicans have charge of the Holy Name Society. St. Thomas Aquinas, often known as the Angelic Doctor, the patron of schools, of Christian philosophy and theology, was a Dominican. Cloistered Dominican Sisters constitute the Second Order. Other Dominican Sisters, as well as many lay folk belong to the Third Order of St. Dominic. There are about 5,000 Dominican Priests and Brothers in the world; about 550 in the United States. Dominican Sisters number several thousands in our country.

Carmelites—These were organized in the year 1151 by St. Berthold, a Franciscan Crusader. St. Simon Stock, through whom the Blessed Virgin gave the world the Brown Scapular, belonged to this Order. Their present house of study in North America is at Niagara Falls, Canada. A separate division is known as the Discalced Carmelities from the time of St. Theresa about 1562. The Little Flower of Jesus, canonized in 1925, belonged to this division. Lay people are affiliated with this organization through the Third Order.

Jesuits—The Society of Jesus, commonly known as the Jesuits, was founded by St. Ignatius Loyola in the year 1540. At present it numbers nearly 20,000 members, of whom nearly 10,000 are priests, and the rest scholastics and Brothers. They conduct universities, colleges, high schools, and have many members in the Foreign Mission Fields.

Redemptorists—The Congregation of the Most Holy Redeemer, or Redemptorists, was founded in 1732 by St. Alphonsus Liguori. The object of the Congregation is principally missionary, although the Fathers are in charge of many parishes.

Passionists—The Congregation of the Most Holy Cross and Passion, or Passionists, were founded by St. Paul of the Cross. Devoted to the most holy Passion of Our Lord, they conduct missions and do parish work. They number about 2,000.

Vincentians—The Congregation of the Mission, known as Lazarists and Vincentians, was founded by St. Vincent de Paul, in 1617. The members were intended to work among the poor and neglected. They conduct missions and retreats, and have engaged in Foreign Mission work. More recently they have charge of parishes. In the United States they number over 400.

Servites—The Order of Servants of Mary, or Servites, was founded in the year 1233 by seven Florentine noblemen. It is a mendicant Order, devoted to preaching and spreading devotion to the Mother of Sorrows. Affiliated with it are cloistered nuns, known as the Second Order. For seculars there is a Third Order.

Congregation of the Holy Cross—The Congregation of the Holy Cross, composed of Priests and Lay Brothers, was established in 1836 by Father Moreau, who united in one organization, the Auxiliary Priests of LeMans and the Brothers of St. Joseph. It comprises the four Provinces of the United States, France, Canada and Bengal, India. Its Superior General resides in the United States. This Congregation has charge of Notre Dame University, of several colleges and many high schools. In this country it numbers about 400 members. It conducts missions here and works in the Bengal Mission field.

Society of the Precious Blood—This Society was founded in 1815 by Blessed Gaspar del Bufalo, in Rome. Its purpose is to conduct missions and retreats. It has three Provinces in Europe and one in the United States, whose membership is nearly 400 divided between Priests, Seminarians and Lay Brothers. It has charge of a college, seminary and about fifty parishes in the United States.

Oblates of Mary Immaculate—The Oblates of Mary, founded a century ago, is spread over the whole world. It numbers fourteen hundred priests. In the United States it has the Northern and Southern Provinces, and a Vive-Province for the French speaking. The priests occupy themselves in preaching Missions, Retreats, and labor in many poor parishes.

Viatorians—This Society was formed in France in 1820, but is named after St. Viator, who lived in the fourth century. It is composed of Priests and Brothers. Their principal purpose is to teach, while they have parishes and preach missions. The American Province counts about one hundred and fifty professed Religious.

Paulists—The Missionary Society of St. Paul the Apostle, or Paulist Fathers, was founded in 1858, by Father Isaac Hecker. Its specific aim is the conversion of non-Catholics. It conducts the Apostolic Mission House near Washington, D.C., and has charge of a number of city parishes. It numbers about 100 members.

Fathers of the Blessed Sacrament—This Congregation was founded in 1856, by Peter Julian Eymard in France. Its Priests and Lay Brothers consecrate their lives to the service of the Blessed Sacrament, and promote devotion to the same by prayer, preaching, and Eucharistic associations. They number 600 members.

Society of the Divine Word—This Society was founded in 1875 by Father Arnold Janssen in Holland. In this short time it has established twenty-seven mission houses in Europe and South America. Its Missionary Priests and Brothers labor in China,

Japan, the Philippines, and elsewhere. The North American Province House is at Techny, Illinois. It numbers 3,000 members.

Marist Fathers—Founded at Lyons, France, by Venerable J. C. Colin, in 1822. It is composed of Priests and Lay Brothers, who cultivate devotion to Mary, and observe the hidden life, though they conduct missions and have charge of colleges. It numbers six Provinces, one of which is in the United States, with headquarters at the Marist Seminary, Washington, D. C.

Marianists—The Society of Mary was founded at Bordeaux in 1817. It is composed of Priests and Brothers who devote themselves to works of education and piety. In America it numbers 600 members.

Religious Brotherhoods—Operating in the United States are several Religious Brotherhoods, some of them having an independent existence, and others forming one organization with Priests by the same name. We have already referred to the latter in conjunction with Religious Orders and Congregations of Priests.

Brothers of the Christian Schools—This Community was founded by St. John Baptist de la Salle in France, in 1679. These Brothers conduct normal schools, colleges, high schools, trading schools, reformatories and orphanages. There are five provinces in the United States.

Little Brother of Mary—This Concregation was founded in France in 1817, to promote primary education. Today it numbers 6,000 members at work in all parts of the world, and conducts a university at Dayton, Ohio.

Xaverian Brothers—This Congregation, founded in Belgium in 1839, conducts six colleges, nine high and seven parochial schools in the United States, and numbers some over 300 members.

Brothers of the Sacred Heart—Founded in France in 1821, this Congregation spread to Spain and Belgium, and finally to the United States, where it conducts grammar and high schools, and orphan asylums.

Alexian Brothers—This Society of men dates back to the fourteenth century, when it was called into being by a wide-spread pestilence. It conducts hospitals in many countries. Its American Novitiate is in Chicago.

PART II

Societies and Organizations

Confraternities are pious associations formally approved by Rome, and usually having an international directive office. Individual branches over all the world participate in the prayers and good works of other branches, and members may gain many Indulgences not accorded to non-members.

Sodality of the Blessed Virgin Mary—This is a pious association of people, both men and women, which has as its object the promotion of devotion to the Blessed Virgin, and the sanctification of members. It was founded as a Jesuit college confraternity in Rome in the year 1563. In the year 1825 Pope Leo XII authorized its introduction in all parishes.

Confraternity of Mount Carmel—Usually on the day of their First Holy Communion, children are enrolled in the Confraternity of Mount Carmel and are invested in what is known as the "Scapular." There are in addition five other Scapulars, namely, those of the Seven Dolors, of the Immaculate Conception, of the Holy Trinity, of The Passion, and of the Sacred Heart.

Confraternity of The Holy Name—Everyone is acquainted with the Holy Name Society, because there are few parishes which have not a branch of it for the male members and there are few cities which have not witnessed a Holy Name Society parade. This Society has a Junior and a Senior division and numbers 1,000,000 members in the United States alone. This Society is seven centuries old and was founded by St. Dominic, to whom the great Dominican Order owes its origin.

The Archconfraternity of The Sacred Heart—The Archconfraternity of the Sacred Heart was established in the year 1830 in Italy. Not identical with the Apostleship of Prayer, all the faithful who belonged to the Apostleship of Prayer before June 7, 1879, belong also to the Archconfraternity and gain its Indulgences. This Confraternity is the outgrowth of the apparition of our Blessed Lord to St. Margaret Mary Alacoque in 1673.

Confraternity of the Holy Rosary—This pious society was started during the lifetime of St. Dominic and has affiliation with the Dominican Order. Parish branches are canonically erected and members are expected to recite the full Rosary of fifteen decades once a week, while no more than five decades on three separate days are required.

Members of the "Living" Rosary unite each with fourteen others to recite the full Rosary daily, each one saying one decade.

Confraternity of Christian Mothers—This Society had its birth at Lille, France, in 1850; was formally instituted in 1856, and was raised to an archconfraternity in 1871, after it had become very popular in Germany. Membership is intended for mothers, who are assisted by direction, prayer and good example in the great work of rearing their children religiously.

The Society for the Propagation of the Faith—In the year 1822 a woman in France conceived the idea of enlisting memberships in a Society which would have as its purpose the spreading of the Faith throughout the world. It crystalized in a movement which was endorsed by Rome, and it was formally approved by Rome as "The Society for the Propagation of the Faith." The new American Republic became one of the first beneficiaries of the funds collected by it.

Today this Society is established in every Christian country, and offers the principal support to Missionary Priests, Sisters and Brothers at work in all pagan lands.

In the United States memberships were solicited on the basis of 5c per month, and since the close of the World War Catholics of this country have contributed as much as all the rest of the world combined. The National Director of the Society in the United States is a member of the Council which meets in Rome at regular intervals for the distribution of the funds. Perpetual memberships for the benefit of foreign missions are $40.00.

In the year 1924 the American Episcopate received the approval of the Holy See to raise the membership fee in the United States to $1.00 per year, in order that 40c from each member might be devoted to the Missions under the American Flag.

At present the Society is known here as the "Society for the Propagation of the Faith for Home and Foreign Missions," and has been introduced into most dioceses. Of the funds collected 60% are sent to the New York Office of the Propagation of the Faith for Foreign Missions and 40% are sent to the Treasurer of the American Board of Catholic Missions for use in our own country.

The Holy Father has granted rich indulgences to all people who affiliate with this joint Society, and grants rare faculties to priests who introduce it and encourage it. Parish promoters write out memberships to every annual contributor of $1.00.

Members are asked to say daily the Our Father and Hail Mary, together with the invocation "St. Francis Xavier, pray for us."

The Catholic Church Extension Society—Organized in 1905 to assist the Home Missions of the United States, the Philippine

Islands, Alaska and Porto Rico. Endorsed by the Holy Father and the American Hierarchy. Assists in building mission churches with donations of $1,000 or more, supplies mission churches with altars, stations of the cross, vestments, chalices, etc. Helps support missionary bishops and priests with subsidies and Mass Intentions. Educates poor students for the missionary priesthood. Supports two Chapel Cars in the mission field. Extension depends entirely upon the voluntary offerings of the faithful for its mission work. Publishes Extension Magazine, the official organ of the Home Missions. Archbishop of Chicago, by his office, presiding officer. Located at 180 North Wabash Avenue, Chicago, Illinois.

The Holy Childhood—The Association of the Holy Childhood is an auxiliary of the Society for the Propagation of the Faith. It is intended for children, from whom, after enrollment, it expects at least one cent per month, and on whom it imposes the easy spiritual burden of reciting once each day one "Hail Mary" and the invocation "Holy Virgin Mary, pray for us and poor pagan children." Perpetual memberships are $25.00.

This Society, started in 1830 by a few students in Paris, has grown to great proportions. Its members are usually united in Parish Conferences, and assist the needy both by money and service, visit the sick, distribute good literature, etc.

Catholic Organizations

The National Catholic Welfare Conference—This is the name applied to an organization which is directed by the Catholic Hierarchy of the United States, principally through an Administrative Committee composed of seven Archbishops and Bishops who are represented by an Executive Secretary at Washington,

D. C., where the Conference has its headquarters, and where annual meetings of the American Episcopate are held.

This organization had its inception in 1917, at the beginning of our entry into World War I, when it was known as the National Catholic War Council.

Under the direction of this organization there are ten Departments, each headed by a Bishop: the Departments, the Executive; of Education; of Laws; of Social Action; of Immigration; of Lay Organizations; of Press and Publicity; of Catholic Action; of the Treasurer and of Finance.

The N.C.W.C. partly subsidizes an International News Service, which has agents in all the capitals of Europe and supplies the service to the Catholic papers of the United States. No secular news agency has correspondents so scholarly and so trustworthy as those of the N.C.W.C.

Knights of Columbus—This fraternal benefit organization for practical Catholic men was founded by the Rev. M. J. McGivney of the Diocese of Hartford, Connecticut, in the year 1882. At this time it has a membership of 500,000 distributed over 2,000 local Councils in every state in the Union, and in Alaska, Canada, Mexico, Hawaii, and the Philippine Islands. Its national headquarters are at New Haven, Connecticut, whence is issued the COLUMBIA, the official monthly magazine of the organization. It has state officers, who are known as State Deputies, and divisions in the state are in charge of a District Deputy, while the presiding officer of local units is called the Grand Knight. Every Council must have a certain number of insurance members, while the majority of members hold social membership only.

The insurance feature of the organization is very attractive because of its soundness from the Actuary viewpoint. The Order has paid out more than $25,000,000 in insurance and has a mortuary reserve fund of $25,000,000.

The Catholic Knights of America—The Catholic Knights of America was founded in the year 1877 as a fraternal insurance organization of Catholic men. Through its parish units it was also tended to promote the spiritual life of its members. Today it has a membership of 20,000. Its insurance is at present on a very sound basis. It has paid out more than $25,000,000 to beneficiaries of nearly 17,000 deceased members. The Catholic Knights have been a strong support of the Catholic Church in America.

The Catholic Order of Foresters (Men)—This Catholic Fraternal Insurance Society originated in Massachusetts in 1879 as a State society. Both men and women belonged to it. In 1883 the Catholic Foresters of Illinois were organized. Then in 1895, after the organization had branches in other states and in Canada, it was made international. Today, it has a membership of 130,000 and a very sane and safe insurance arrangement.

The Catholic Order of Foresters (Women)—The Women's Catholic Order of Foresters was organized in Chicago in 1892. It is now established in most states as an Assessment Life Insurance and Benevolent organization and has a membership of 65,000.

Ancient Order of Hibernians—The origin of this Order is traced to the 16th century when Catholics were bitterly persecuted in Ireland. It was established in this country in the year 1836. Membership is limited to Catholics who are of Irish birth or Irish descent and of good moral character. Its motto is: "Friendship, Unity, and True Christian Charity." The Order aims at advancing the principles of Irish nationality and it supports the aged and sick members. It also offers funeral benefits. **Before the**

World War it had a membership exceeding 130,000, in the United States, Canada and Hawaii. Some years ago it presented the Catholic University of America with $50,000 to found a "Chair of Irish History."

A Ladies' Auxiliary to this Order was established at Omaha, Nebraska, in 1894. It has had its own National Officers since 1906, and its membership has grown to 60,000. The Ladies contributed $10,000 towards a Scholarship at Trinity College, Washington, D. C.

Catholic Benevolent Legion—This Fraternal Assessment Insurance Society was organized in Brooklyn in 1881. It has the same social and benevolent aims as other Catholic organizations. Its maximum membership was about 25,000, while it has paid out nearly $25,000,000 in benefits.

Young Men's Institute—This is a fraternal organization founded in 1883, at San Francisco. Its purpose is to bestow aid and sick benefits, and to improve its members morally, socially and intellectually. Its motto is "For God and for Country." Its membership, divided among beneficiary, active and honorary, reached about 20,000 in the United States and its possessions, and in Canada.

Catholic Daughters of America—This organization originally chartered in New York as the Daughters of Isabella changed its name because of friction with an organization of the same name previously founded in Connecticut. Its aims are similar to those of the Daughters of Isabella. It has expanded, and at present has a membership of 150,000. At is annual conventions the delegates vote considerable assistance to different works of charity and religion. The National Shrine to Mary Immaculate, Washington, and the National Catholic School of Social Service, among other worthy causes, have been beneficiaries of its zeal and charity.

Daughters of Isabella—This organization, as now constituted, is officially known as the National Circle Daughters of Isabella. It had its origin in Connecticut.

It admits white women between the ages of sixteen and sixty, who are practical Catholics, and its purpose is to render assistance to the sick and distressed members or to the beneficiaries of such members by the payment of sick and funeral benefits, and to promote social and intellectual intercourse among its members. The organization has done considerable for the Missions and charity. The National Circle has endowed a scholarship at the National Catholic School of Social Service conducted under the auspices of the N.C.W.C. The membership in 1927 was 35,000.

Central Verein—The Central Verein of North America dates back to 1855. It is intended for people of German birth or descent, and its object is to promote a zealous Catholic laity and to oppose social evils and the growth of forbidden, secret societies. The organization has a membership of 100,000 distributed over State Leagues in this commonwealth.

This organization established the Leo House in New York for the care of Catholic immigrants, founded a Teachers' Seminary at St. Francis, Wisconsin, and has been a great advocate of sound Christian education. Its headquarters are, at present, at St. Louis, where it publishes considerable literature. At the 1927 convention it voted $250,000 to carry on social service work.

Catholics in the World Number 349,000,000

The (Roman) Catholic population of the world is estimated at 348,617,231. The Continental distribution is as follows:

Europe: Latin Rite, 203,367,579; Rites other than Latin, 5,514,019; Total Catholics 208,881,598.

*Asia: Latin Rite, 15,635,812; Rites other than Latin, 900,-000; Total Catholics, 16,535,812.

Africa: Latin Rite, 5,289,445; Rites other than Latin, 40,000; Total Catholics, 5,329,445.

America: Latin Rite, 115,190,446; Rites other than Latin, 600,000; Total Catholics, 115,790,446.

Australia: Latin Rite, 2,070,930; Total Catholics, 2,070,930.

Totals:

Latin Rite 341,563,579

Rites other than Latin   7,054,019

Total Catholics 348,617,231
*Includes Philippines.

It is estimated that there are about 315,000 priests in the world.

Number of Oriental Catholics—While most Catholics belong to the Latin rite, there are, especially in the so-called Near East, some 8,000,000, whose liturgical services, including the Mass, are performed according to a different rite and in a different language. In fact, there are in all nineteen different rites, as follows:

Latin, Mozarabic, Ambrosian, Chaldean, Malabar, Coptic, Abyssinian, Pure Syriac, Armenian, Maronite, Pure Greek, Italo-Greek, Georgian, Melchite, Bulgarian, Serbian, Rumanian, Russian, and Ruthenian.

CHAPTER FIVE

What Roman Catholics Believe in a Roman Catholic Country

The information given in this chapter will be a revelation, not only to non-Catholics, but also to many American Catholics. The Church of Rome does not reveal all its invention in Protestant countries.

Many cannot understand how an individual in his right mind can believe the teachings of Romanism. In defense of many Roman Catholics of good faith, I must say that it is not a belief, but an acceptance, since a Roman Catholic is not permitted to question the doctrines of his church.

But it takes a long time to induce a nation of people to give up the Godgiven right of investigation. However after several centuries of Romanism in Europe and Latin-American countries, the pope and priests are now able to impose their authority on the minds of the people to the extent that it seems extremely presumptuous to them for a person to question Roman Catholic dogmas.

In America Roman officials are very careful in introducing

their novelties. They reveal them one by one. They know that American Catholics, because of the beneficent influence of Protestantism and the love of freedom, are not yet ready to accept Catholic teaching about relics, saints, and the supposed miracles of saints without investigation. They also know that these things can never stand a national investigation.

The publicity officials and mass psychologists of Rome have considered it more practical to start with Mary. Even we Protestants have great respect for Mary because she was the mother of Jesus. But Roman Catholics are told that Mary is the mother of God, because Jesus was divine. She is presented as the "Queen of Heaven," and Catholics are told she can do everything for us. What Jesus will not do in answer to our petition, He will do if we send His mother to ask a favor in our name. With this established in Catholic minds, it is easy to bring them to believe that Mary is able to take souls out of Purgatory. Thus arose the teaching of the Scapular.

The dogma of the Scapular was introduced a long time ago in America. Therefore American Roman Catholics now accept it without question. They never seem to wonder how Mary can go once a week on Saturday to free those who wore her Scapular, when she should go at least twice a week; since when it is Saturday in China it is not Saturday in America. Nor do they stop to consider what will happen to one who dies on Saturday night at 11 P.M. where there is Daylight Saving Time, since it will be Saturday according to Standard Time, but Sunday according to Daylight Saving Time. Will Mary take him out before 12 P.M. or a week later?

While the devotion of the Scapular of Our Lady of Mt. Carmel was advertised in America long ago and acceptance was made easy by the propaganda of those Roman Catholics who immigrated from Europe with stories about the weeping Madonna, apparitions to children, etc., yet acceptance on a national scale came only in the second part of the twentieth century. To create more interest in America, where people are more practical and less speculative, Roman psychologists decided to present Mary as the Saviour of Modern Civilization against Russia. Communism was presented as a great evil that only the Mother of God can defeat. Thus devotion to Mary has become very popular in America. Later we will see more of the devotion of Our Lady of Fatima.

Only when American Roman Catholics have been thoroughly trained in Maryolatry will Rome introduce the Saints.

But in Europe, as I have said, it is different. Let us see, therefore, what Roman Catholics in Europe are willing to accept. In doing this we will also see the kind of teachings Rome will eventually introduce in America according to a master plan to create a Roman Catholic mind in this country. The creation of a Roman Catholic mind in America does not involve the conversion of non-Catholics and Protestants to Romanism. It means the use of all means of publicity to present Catholic doctrines and inventions throughout the nation so as to bring Roman Catholics to an absolute acceptance of them and to cause others to lose the sense of revolt and pity. They think universal publicity will bring Americans to contemplate Romanism without mental insult. If Roman Catholics succeed in their master plan, then freedom-loving Americans and especially Protestants had as well move to the Dark Continent.

Roman Catholics of Europe accept and venerate as genuine the following relics:

THE BLOOD OF CHRIST: In 1247 a portion of the Saviour's blood was presented to the king of England in a beautiful crystalline vessel and carried by him with great reverence to Westminster. The Bishop of Norwich preached a sermon explaining its glories and promising that "Whoever worshipped this most holy blood would, by the permission of the prelates, obtain free remission of penances for six years and a hundred and forty days" (Matt. Paris, at A.D. 1247).

We do not need to kneel down in front of the portion of the Saviour's blood to obtain remission of sins, since the Holy Word tells us "The blood of Jesus Christ, his Son, cleanses us from all sins," I John 1:7—from all sins and without limitation of time.

THE TRUE CROSS: This is the most famous of all the relics ever worshipped and they say it was found by Helena, the mother of Constantine the Great, in the fourth century.

The Roman Catholic 'Question Box' by the Paulist Fathers, N. Y., N. Y. on page 374 admits that "Whether St. Helena herself discovered the True Cross may be questioned." "The grave improbability, and even impossibility, of the story appears from the following considerations. (1) For three centuries the cross had disappeared, and there is no record in history of its having been preserved either by the friends or the enemies of Christ; the apostles never referred to it. (2) No historical evidence was produced at the time to establish its identity. Eusebius, the historian, a contemporary, made no mention of the finding of it. (3) The cross, if buried where it is said to have been found, must in the course of three hundred years have either decayed or been destroyed in the destruction of the city; moreover, the place where it is said to have been found was in the center of the modern city, whereas both Calvary and the sepulchre were outside the city." John McDonald, B.D. in 'Romanism Analysed' Scottish Reform. Society, Edinburgh.

While Roman Catholics claim not to worship, but only to venerate saints, images and relics—cult of DULIA—they admit to worship "adore" the "nails and wood" of the cross. In the Roman Missal, rubric for Good Friday, we read: ". . . Then he (the priest) proceeds to the middle of the altar, and totally uncovering the cross and elevating it, he begins a third time more loudly, 'Behold the Wood of the Cross upon which the salvation of the world hangs. Come, let us *adore*' Then taking off his shoes *he approaches to adore the cross, thrice kneeling, before he kisses it*. When he has done this he returns, and puts on his shoes; and afterwards the ministers of the altars, and then the other clergy, and laity, two by two thrice kneeling, as is before said, *adore the cross*."

Again in the Roman Missal on the feast of the "Exaltation of the Cross," September 14, we read:

" 'O cross, more splendid than all the stars, etc., Sweet Wood, sweet nails, bearing a sweet burden, save the present multitude assembled today in thy praise.' Then the Pontiff (the officiating priest) kneeling before the cross devoutly adores and kisses it (*Ipsam devote adorat et osculatur*). The same all others who wish may do."

The above act of adoration is given not only to the True Cross, but to all the crosses and crucifixes.

The following places claim to possess the True Cross or a great portion of it: Jerusalem, Persia, Constantinople, England, France, Venice and Rome, in the Basilica of St. Cross.

THE SAVIOUR'S DRESS: Venice, Italy, claims to possess a portion of the True Cross with a part of the Saviour's dress, and some of the earth which imbibed his blood.

NAILS AND THORNS: In the year 938 King Athelstan of England received as gifts a piece of the True Cross, a small portion of the crown of thorns, and the sword of Constantine the Great, on the hilt of which, upon thick plates of gold, was fastened one of the four nails used to crucify Christ, so it is said.

THE SWORD WHICH PIERCED THE BODY OF CHRIST: In the year 1089 Peter of Provence had a vision from Saint Andrew, who told him three times to go to the church of St. Peter in Antioch where he would discover the sword which pierced the body of Christ. The sword, they say, was discovered and the people hearing the glad news, "flocked to the church and worshipped so precious relic." (Matt. Paris, at A.D. 1089.)

THE COAT OF CHRIST: This goes under the name of of "The Holy Coat of Treves," which is said to be the seamless coat of Christ, for which the soldiers cast lots. Mary, it is said, made this robe when Christ was still young and it enlarged itself as He grew.

John McDonald, B. D., makes the following comment in his book mentioned before:

"Q. 9. What relic has created great interest among Romanists in recent years?

A. "The Holy Coat of Treves," which is said to be the seamless coat of Christ, for which the soldiers cast lots. Like the cross, it is said to have been discovered by Helena about 325.

Q. 10. Is it held in high esteem by the Church of Rome?

A. It is held in such high esteem that in 1891 Leo XIII promised "complete absolution and remission of all sins," and "the remission of seven years of the penance imposed on them or otherwise due by them," to all pilgrims who would visit the church during the exhibition of the garment and pray for the extirpation of erroneous doctrines. (*Standard,* August 17th, 19th, 1891.) So popular was the relic that hundreds of thousands visited it during the six weeks it was on view, and many of them were heard to pray as they passed, "Holy Coat, save me! Holy Coat, pray for me and protect me!" So great was the rush of the faithful that the railway company erected three new temporary stations, the tramway company laid down two new sets of rails, and licenses were asked for one thousand three hundred new temporary beer saloons and public houses!

Q. 11. Mention any facts disproving the genuineness of this relic.

A. (1) It is one of twenty-two coats, all of which claim to be, and are actually adored as, Christ's seamless coat: of these there is one at St. Croce, and another at St. Praxede's, in Rome. (2) It has a special rival at Argentuil in France, which, equally with itself, received the authentification of a Pope: the Bull of Pope Leo X decided in favor of the Treves coat, and the Brief of Pope Gregory XVI in favor of the Argentuil coat, while a third Pope, Urban VIII, authenticated both. (3) An examination of the coat by experts in 1844 brought to light unfavorable facts: the length of the garment—five feet; its color—purple; its material—soft and silken, like fine linen; its structure—not woven but knit, and the presence of figures worked in the substance of it, all prove that the tunic is not only not such a garment as Christ would have worn, but not a Palestine garment at all. ("Dublin University Magazine," Nov. 1845, p. 518.)

Q. 12. Do the Romish authorities grant the members of the Church full liberty to discuss the value of such relics?

A. No; they prohibit it when they have the power. The city authorities of Treves forbade discussion under the most severe penalties, and one newspaper editor was committed to prison for fourteen days for writing disparagingly of the coat.

Q. 13. Was the Treves relic credited with miraculous power, or turned to lucrative uses?

A. Yes. To attract the faithful on the last occasion of its exhibition, the bishop quoted the assurance of his predecessor, "that the Almighty Himself, through many miraculous cures, had notified to the world how acceptable the devotion to the Holy Coat was to Him." (*Tablet,* 25th July, 1891.) He also sought alms "to assist, first, in mitigating the distress of the Pope, and secondly, to help in restoring the Cathedral of Treves"; from which appeal he reaped a rich harvest.

THE TRUE PICTURE OF CHRIST: It is said that Veronica was a saint of Jerusalem at the time of Christ who, seeing Jesus pass on his way to be crucified, his brow covered with blood and his face saddened by suffering, removed the sash or scarf which constituted a part of her turban and gave it to the fainting Saviour, that he might wipe his bleeding brow. In return for her kindness, the scarf was handed back to her containing a likeness of the Saviour, disfigured as he was by suffering and saddened by sorrow. This relic is held in great veneration in St. Peter's in Rome. Veronica, who is considered a saint by the church of Rome, never existed, her name was formed by blundering and uniting the two words *vera ico* (true image), which the first impostor wrote on the painting of the supposed Saviour's image.

THE HOLY STAIRS: One of the great attractions of the *basilica of St. John Lateran* is "the Holy Stairs," consisting of 28 marble steps, traditionally declared to have belonged to

Pilate's house, and to have been sanctified by being ascended and descended by our Saviour at the time of his trial; now kept under a portico on the north side of the basilica, preserved from further wear by being covered with planks, and allowed to be ascended by penitents only on their knees. When Martin Luther was humbly creeping up these stairs, he thought he heard a voice of thunder in his heart, crying, "The just shall live by faith"; and in amazement and shame he rose from his knees, and fled from the basilica.

In spite of the progress of the twentieth century pilgrims still ascend the worn marble stairs, devoutly kissing each step as they approach it in order to gain indulgences. The stairs were brought through the air, as Roman Catholics believe, ages ago, to Rome.

THE CRIB OF JESUS: The gorgeous chapel in the right aisle of the *Basilica of Santa Maria Maggiore* in Rome, built by Pope Sixtus V, and called the Sistine chapel or chapel of the Holy Sacrament, is magnificently adorned, and has in its center the smaller chapel of the *Praesepe* (manger, or crib), where is preserved the sacred crib or cradle, consisting of five boards of the manger in which the infant Jesus is said to have been deposited at his birth, inclosed in an urn of silver and crystal with a fine gilt figure of the child on the top. On Christmas eve thousands of Roman Catholics take part (to) in a solemn ceremony and procession.

A GARMENT OF THE VIRGIN MARY: Charles the Bald, it is said, brought to France from Constantinople a certain linen belonging to Mary. It is now venerated at Chartres, France.

THE HAIR OF THE VIRGIN MARY: Some of the hair of Mary, enclosed in a gold box are in England given by Turketul, abbot of Croyland, to his brethren monks in the year 975.

THE CHAINS OF ST. PETER: The chain is about two yards long, and the rings are large and rusty looking. It was found in Jerusalem, it is said, and presented by the Empress Eudoxia to Pope Leo I. He had in his possession another chain, the one with which Peter had been bound in Rome by Nero, and when he brought his chain near to the one which bound Peter in Jerusalem when the angel set him free, immediately they leaped together and were at once perfectly and miraculously united. Next to the chains there is a contribution box with these words written on it: "Alms for the cult of the venerable chains."

CHAIR OF ST. PETER: A Superb shrine of gilt bronze, supported by four gigantic figures of the same materials, representing the four doctors of the church, St. Augustine, St. Ambrose, St. Athanasius (or St. Jerome) and St. John Chrysostom, closes the view of the nave of St. Peter's church. The shrine is in the form of a throne, and contains a chair which Peter occupied, it is said, as bishop of Rome. It was given to Peter by a wealthy Roman senator.

THE HEAD OF ST. JOHN THE BAPTIST: It was discovered, it is said, by some monks of the Macedonian sect during the reign of emperor Valens, who commanded that it should be brought to Constantinople. But the mules drawing the carriage in which there was the head of St. John, stopped at Pantichium, in Chalcedonia, and no lashing and coaxing could move them one step farther. The emperor Theodosius, prompted by an impulse of God, was able to remove it to a place in the suburbs of Constantinople, where he erected for it a magnificent church. Matthey Paris, an English Roman Catholic monk and a historian tells us of a head of St. John the Baptist, *a second one*, which was taken to Edessa in the year 761.

THE HEAD OF ST. LUKE: The head of St. Luke, together with the arm of St. Andrew, was brought to Rome by Gregory the Great before he became the pope and given as gifts to his monastery of St. Andrew in Rome.

THE FEATHER OF THE ANGEL GABRIEL, THE BOTTLE OF THE VIRGIN MARY'S MILK, THE TEARS OF OUR SAVIOUR are preserved in the chapel of the Scala Sancta in Rome.

THE SHEET OF CHRIST: The linen cloth in which the body of Christ was wrapped in the sepulchre, containing the likeness of his whole body, is preserved at Turin, Italy, in the Royal Chapel, property of the Royal House of Italy. Roman Catholics are permitted to see the sheet (Sindone) only during the Holy Week.

Relics of almost every possible description are said to exist, and priests have been led into the absurd and impossible by their zeal to increase their number and variety. There are six seamless garments, each claiming to be genuine. At one time there were thirteen heads, all said to have belonged to John the Baptist. Eight heads were attributed to Stephen, the first Christian martyr. James the Great had ten. In the same way there are five complete bodies of Andrew and eight of Luke.

There is a story that a tourist on being shown a second head of John the Baptist, asked for an explanation of the anomaly, and the sacristan replied: "Oh! but what you saw before was his head as a boy, while this is his head when he was a man."

The body of the Apostle Bartholomew is declared in the Roman breviary and martyrology to have been translated from

Benevento to Rome by the Emperor Otto III (983-1002), and is declared to be entire. It is attested by bulls of Alexander III and Sixtus V, but the church of Benevento alleges that the entire body of St. Bartholomew is there still, and produces bulls to that effect from Leo IX, Stephen IX, Benedict XII, Clement VI, Boniface IX, and Urban V, the earliest of which popes reigned fifty years after the death of Otto III. Here then are two entire bodies; but Monte Casino claims the possession of a larger part of the body, and so does Reims. There are besides three heads, one at Naples, one formerly at Reichenau, and a third at Toulouse; two crowns of the head at Frankfort and Prague; part of the skull at Maestricht; a jaw at Steinfeld, part of a jaw at Prague, two jaws in Cologne, and a lower jaw at Murbach; an arm and hand at Gersiac; a second arm, with the flesh, at Bethune; a third arm at Amalfi; a large part of a fourth arm at Foppens; a fifth arm and part of a sixth at Cologne; a seventh arm at Andechs; an eighth arm at Ebers; three large leg or arm bones in Prague; part of an arm at Brussels; and other alleged portions of the body, not to speak of trifles like skin, teeth, and hair, in twenty other places.

Forty nails used in the crucifixion of the Saviour are claimed by Catholic churches, all declared authentic by the possessors. Of course, only three, or at most four, could have been used.

A handkerchief worn by Mary; the halter with which Judas hung himself; the wedding ring of the Virgin; a piece of Jacob's ladder; a part of the "swaddling clothes" in which Mary wrapped the infant Jesus; the brazen serpent which Moses lifted up in the wilderness (which Hezekiah destroyed); the head of John the Baptist in several different churches; bits of the bodies of eleven of the children slain by Herod in Bethlehem; a bottle of Joseph's breath, caught and preserved by an angel while Joseph was cutting wood; the tail of the ass on which

Christ made his triumphant entry into Jerusalem, which was held in the greatest esteem and venerated by the Dominican Fathers at Genoa, who instituted a festival and ordered a mass in honor of the ass; parts of the bodies of many saints, Abraham, Daniel, Jonah, Zechariah, Bartholomew, Peter, James, Paul, and others too numerous to mention; a bottle of Egyptian darkness.

Some earth from the desert where Christ fed the five thousand; a piece of the tomb of Lazarus; a lock of the Virgin's hair; a portion of the original copy of the Pentateuch as written by Ezra; the table at which Christ and the apostles reclined when the Lord's Supper was instituted; a part of the Virgin's veil; some earth from the spot on the mountain in Galilee where Christ appeared to "above five hundred brethren at once"; the porphyry slab on which the soldiers cast lots for the seamless garment of Christ; five boards from the Saviour's manger; the first shirt he ever wore; the finger of Thomas, which the Saviour told him to "reach hither" and put into the print of the nails; the title which Pilate wrote and put on the cross; the waterpots used at the marriage in Cana of Galilee, and some of the wine; a stone on which Peter knelt to pray when he saw Simon Magus carried off by demons, and which still bears the prints of his knees; the marble slab on which Paul was beheaded; a piece of the tomb of Christ; the column to which Jesus was bound when beaten with rods; the shoes which He wore when a boy; a piece of the Saviour's girdle; a picture of Christ which Peter gave to Pudens; a part of the reed and sponge used at the crucifixion; a piece of the towel with which Christ wiped the apostles' feet; a part of the Saviour's seamless robe; so many bottles of the Virgin's milk, that, as Calvin says, "had the breasts of the Most Holy Virgin yielded a more copious supply than is given by a cow, and had she continued to nurse during her whole life-time, she could scarcely have furnished the quantity which is exhibited."

THE BLOOD OF ST. JANUARIUS: Saint Januarius, the patron saint of Naples, is practically the god of that great city, with its six hundred thousand inhabitants. Everywhere he is honored and worshiped as the presiding divinity of the place. The cathedral of Naples is dedicated to him. This cathedral contains a wonderful little chapel, which cost over a million dollars, and this also is dedicated to the "Divine Januarius." It was erected in consequence of a vow made to St. Januarius during the plague of 1527, it being understood that if he would stop the plague the people would build the chapel. Many wonderful things are related concerning this saint.

Three of the great annual festivals of Naples honor the occasion of the so-called liquefaction of the blood of St. Januarius, which blood the priests profess to have in a small vial. This miraculous liquefaction takes place three times a year, on his feast days, September 19th and December 20th, that the people may have an undeniable demonstration of the fact that their patron saint is still alive and zealously guarding the interest of the city. If this so-called miracle fails to take place at the appointed time, many of the people become nervous and anxious, fearing that something has happened to displease St. Januarius, and that he may thus refuse to hear their prayers and avert the evils that are liable to befall them at any time. What power this gives the priests!

Years ago, when the French entered Naples and took possession of the city, the archbishop announced to the people that St. Januarius was greatly displeased at the presence of these foreign invaders in the city, for the blood would not liquefy at the appointed time. Hearing of this, and knowing how disastrous it might prove to his cause, the French general quietly sent a messenger to the archbishop to say to him that if the blood were not liquefied within twenty-four hours he would burn the cathedral to the ground. It is needless to say that the miracle (?) was soon performed and announced to the people, who little suspected the real cause. (For more information read "Echoes of Europe" by E. K. Washington.)

THE HOUSE OF CHRIST: Better known under the name of Holy House of Loreto. Italy is full of shrines, places that lay claim to special sanctity, and wonderful miracles, where pilgrims are said to acquire special merit and indulgences. Some of them are only known in their immediate territory, but others have acquired even an international reputation. Among the many that might be mentioned, none perhaps is better known than the so-called Holy House of Loreto, which for six hundred years has been an object of veneration in Italy and has proved a rich mine of gold for the church. It has been visited by millions of pilgrims, including kings and queens, popes and princes, and many other titled folk. Benito Mussolini donated this gold-mine sanctuary to the Vatican, together with the Sanctuary of St. Anthony of Padua.

At the end of the nineteenth century this famous sanctuary was visited by James Jackson Jarves, an American art critic, who spent many years in Italy. I am transcribing a portion of his account, given in his book *Italian Rambles,* and reproduced also by J. H. Eager, D. D. in *Romanism In Its Home,* American Baptist Publication, Philadelphia, Pennsylvania.

Descending the hill of Recanati toward the Adriatic for about three miles, we come to another, lower town, terminating in a gentle swell, on the summit of which is the stately church and outbuildings of the Madonna of Loreto. The town itself is a compactly built suburb of the sanctuary, living on the traffic produced by the numerous pilgrims of all nations who frequent this shrine during the warm months. The main group of buildings, with the pontifical palace and its long portico, are imposing, and in the Bramante style of architecture. Especially noticeable for their artistic beauty are the bronze doors of the church and the fountain in the piazza in front, executed by the brothers Lombardi, Bernardini, and Vercelli, in the sixteenth century. Entering the church the central attraction is the beautiful marble case or covering in the form of a diminutive palace, covered with statues and bas reliefs, begun by Sansonino and terminated by Sangallo and the ablest architects and sculptors and bronzists of the sixteenth century of the classical Renaissance. It was made after the design of Bramante, at an enormous expense. In itself it is a gem of art. But to the pilgrims its sole value is in its being the honorable shield or cover which protects the outer walls of the Casa Santa, or holy house, which was once the residence of the Virgin Mary at Nazareth, in Palestine. It consists of a single room of rude masonry, about fifteen feet long by twelve wide, the flat stones, bricks or pieces of marble being laid in three courses a foot and a half thick, with considerable intervening mortar. A little book purporting to be the authentic history of the holy house, as sanctioned by the Roman Church, is sold to visitors, and from it I take the following brief statement.

"In this simple apartment the Virgin lived with Jesus until he grew to manhood and departed on his mission. After the crucifixion she remained in it until her death, frequently visited by the apostles and other disciples of Jesus.

When Nazareth was pillaged by the soldiers of **Vespasian,** the house of Mary was miraculously preserved. They could not enter the lane where it was situated or touch its walls, which God preserved to make one day an object of worship for all Christians." So the book states.

After this time it became a center of pilgrimage for the faithful everywhere. St. Helena, mother of Constantine the Great, found it intact in the ruins of the town," "unsullied by the worship of idols." She was not disposed to trust it longer solely to miraculous care, so she surrounded it with massive walls and iron railings, in the form of a magnificent catacomb or temple. In this state it remained an object of devotion to the Christian world until Palestine was overrun by the Saracens and the edifice of St. Helena destroyed by them. This was A. D. 1291. The Almighty again directly interfered to preserve it. By the hands of His angels He detached it from its foundations, "which remain today to attest the fact," and carried it on their shoulders across the seas to Dalmatia, depositing it on a hill near the coast called Raunizza.

Not trusting wholly to description to make this miracle sensible to the pious readers, the author gives a picture of the scene as witnessed by many spectators at the moment of its aerial voyage. The Madonna, holding the infant Jesus in her arms, is seated on the sharp pitch of the roof, while boy and adult angels are lifting and escorting the stone cabin, in a blaze of celestial light, in its rapid flight over land and sea. Naturally the peasants are astonished to see a building in the "form of a church with a tower and two bells on the roof hanging over their heads with no support of foundation or floor." In the interior they saw an altar with a crucifix painted on cloth attached to a cedar plank, and a statue also of cedar, of the blessed Virgin and her Son, with their hair and clothes fashioned in the style of Nazareth, and an old dilapidated wardrobe. "A miracle was evident, but it was an enigma for all," until the Virgin herself, in a vision to the curé of the neighborhood, explained the "great secret." "The house was that in which she was born, lived, was saluted by the angel, conceived of the Divine Word, and where she nursed and raised the infant God."

The Dalmatians gave a cordial welcome to the Casa Salynta, devoutly worshiped it, provided for its preservation and the comfort of the pilgrims it attracted, and were prospering greatly in their worldly estates, when to their intense chagrin and monetary loss, after a stay of only three years and seven months, without warning or reason, it flew over the sea and lodged itself in a grove of laurels, two miles from the coast, near its present site. The bereaved inhabitants took such comfort as they could get in putting up the following brief inscription in its place: "The Holy House of the Virgin came to Tersatto May 10, 1291, and left December 10, 1294," without further comment. In their prayers, however, they were wont, for a long period, to ejacuate in tears: "Return to us, O beautiful lady; come back to us, O Mary, with your house." But it would not come.

In its new locality the Virgin appeared again in dreams to various pious individuals to attest the authenticity of the building and the genuineness of the miracle. But it would appear that in its hasty flight and lighting, it had not sufficiently considered the character of the neighborhood. There were no accommodations for the devout pilgrims, or food. The richest and most delicate visitors had to sleep on the bare earth and subsist as they best might. There were no roads, and to make matters worse, "the prince of darkness, jealous of the holy house, sent bands of robbers to spoil and kill its visitors," to such a degree that soon put a stop to them, and it was left quite alone in the society of thieves and murderers.

Being of a social as well as moral disposition, the house after an eight months' trial of its new home, rose again in the air, and planted itself a little more inland in a verdant hill near Recanati.

The owners of this site were two brothers, who were greatly pleased at an event which gave so much additional value to their estate. Pilgrims came again by thousands, bringing gifts, greatly to their benefit. At the sight of so much riches flowing to them, they became very avaricious and quarreled over the division, nigh unto killing each other. "The Most High," I quote literally, "irritated at this fraternal discord, suddenly withdrew the house of His divine mother and transferred it to another charming hill, near-by, where it still remains," much to the edification and benefit of the people who make up the motley population of Loreto.

I did not see the old wardrobe of the Virgin, perhaps because it was too much encased in jewels, but I was shown a little earthen porringer, or bowl, encased in solid gold, beautifully wrought in relief, out of which the little Jesus was accustomed to be fed when weaned. I also saw the black, ugly image of the Madonna and Bambino carved by St. Luke,—his being a sculptor as well as painter was new to me,—or as much of it as the intense blaze of diamonds, sapphires, rubies, emeralds, and other precious stones, in which it was literally encased, would admit; the biggest diamond being the gift of the sainted Antonelli, and a glorious sight it was for a lover of precious stones, or a lady of fashion, barring the covetous feelings they might incite in their misplaced position.

These treasures are the accumulated gifts of the present century only, the French in the last having made a clean sweep of precious gifts of royal personages and the devout, wealthy pilgrims, to the amount of many millions of dollars. So rapidly, however, do they accumulate that even in our unbelieving time, since 1792, the vast hall or chapel of the treasure has been refilled with precious gifts—largely jewelry—but by no means of equal to the former gifts of which it had been despoiled in the preceding century.

The Casa Santa is also very richly endowed in lands. The greatest Catholic potentates and highest prelates, both of Europe and America, give their sanction by visits, gifts, and devotion to the stupidly contrived tale which brings so much wealth to this shrine and makes it a fertile nursery of an imbecile kind of devotion destructive to real religion. Millions of lips have kissed and licked in spots the rough surfaces of the interior stone wall of the house, until they are as smooth and glistening as plate glass; millions also have kissed and licked the bronze figure in relief of the scourged Christ on one of the doors, until it is all worn down to a thin, shapeless outline; millions of bare knees, in making the circuit of the marble foundations of the outer walls in penance, have worn deep channels in the stone, and it is said that many pilgrims go up the long hill that leads to the church on their knees, kissing and licking the earth and stones as they drag themselves slowly onward.

The crowds are taught to believe that the Casa Santa miraculously converts heretics and Jews; that it cures diseases, saves sinners; that it stops earthquakes, epidemics, wars; that Mary of Loreto always grants the petitions of her worshipers here, and that the district of Piceno under auspicious protection, is proof against all dangers and disaster; and this they believe, though a few years since, in sight of the shrine, General Cialdini defeated the papal forces under General Lamoriciere and won the Marches and Loreto itself for the hated kingdom of Italy. Since these events there has been improvement even here— more cleanliness, fewer beggars, no brigands, and the opportunity of wholesome progress. Nevertheless, Italians say, the nearer you get to the great sanctuary the worse is the blasphemy in which so many Italians are adepts, the more cheating and pilfering, and they give the neighborhood a bad name, calling it a gospel shop, where religion is made a mere traffic. Personally I noticed nothing specially reprehensible or differing from Catholic shrines generally.

In the figure of an aged servant of the church, in the uniform of an invalid soldier, on guard at the door of the holy house, with a diminutive drawn cutlass, presenting arms to every priestly visitor in a very solemn manner, while punching or shoving aside the poor ones, there was a touch of the ridiculous. He was so weak in every joint, and so unwarlike in every gesture, and had such a piteous, not felonious but fee-pleading look, that he interested me far more than St. Luke's Virgin and her diamonds or the earthern porringer. If they would only write him down in the veritable history as the Blessed Virgin's old family servant, miraculously preserved with the house, millions would swallow this statement as readily as the other.

CHAPTER SIX

What Roman Catholics Believe in a Non-Roman Catholic Country

Two Major Devotions

Roman Catholic officials know very well that the Roman Catholics in America will not go for the "two heads of St. John" or the "bottles of milk of Mary." There is too much Protestant influence and too many intelligent people in the U.S.A. to suit Romanism. Therefore little is said about relics in Roman Catholic literature for American consumption.

While the Church of Rome had to invent thousands upon thousands of relics and devotions in order to please the individualistic and campanilistic spirit of the Europeans and to get them to pour out their money, over here in America people go more for a national attraction than for a local one. Therefore instead of multiplying the devotions, a particular one for each town, as in Europe, priests are capitalizing very well on two major devotions: Our Lady of the Scapular of Mt. Carmel, and Madonna of Fatima.

SCAPULAR OF MARY OF MT. CARMEL

"In the year 1245, St. Simon Stock was chosen general of the order of the Blessed Virgin Mary of Mount Carmel. This holy man was born in the country of Kent, in the year 1163. When he was twelve years of age, he withdrew himself into a wood, where he lived for the space of twenty years in great austerity, and in the perpetual exercise of celestial meditations, having for his house the trunk of a hollow oak, from whence he was named Stock, and had for his food: roots, herbs, and sometimes bread, which a dog brought him in his mouth, especially on festival days.

As he was upon his knees in the oratory, the most glorious Virgin, environed with celestial splendour in the company of many thousands of angels, appeared to him, and holding the sacred Scapular in her hand, she said to him these words: *Receive, most beloved Son, the Scapular of thy Order, a sign of my confraternity, a privilege both to thee and to all Carmelites, in which he that dieth shall not suffer eternal fire; behold the sign of salvation, a safeguard in danger, the covenant of peace, and everlasting alliance.*

In the ensuing seven centuries, this increasingly, celebrated *Scapular Promise* was studied and found theologically sound; questioned, and was confirmed by miracles . . . so numerous, said Blessed Claude de la Colombiére, S. J., "That no devotion has been confirmed with miracles more numerous and authentic."

Since the nucleus of this vast Confraternity is the Carmelite Order, it is interesting to note:

The Carmelites derive their name from Mount Carmel, in Palestine, where, as is traditionally believed, the forefathers of the Order, descendants from the Prophet Elias, were visited by Our Lady during Her lifetime on earth.

The first public oratory ever erected on earth in honor of Our Lady was erected by these monks, according to the oldest traditions.

The gift of the Scapular universalized the Carmelite Order as "Our Lady's Family," as Pius IX explained: "This most extraordinary gift of the Scapular . . . from the Mother of God to Saint Simon Stock . . . brings its great usefulness not only to the Carmelite Family of Mary but also to all the rest of the faithful who wish, affiliated to that Family, to follow Mary with a very special devotion."

The prime reward of the Scapular devotion is *Assurance of Salvation,* granted by Our Lady in the already quoted promise: "Whosoever dies clothed in this (Scapular) *shall not suffer eternal fire!*

For this reward, two conditions must be fulfilled: one must be lawfully enrolled into the Scapular Confraternity, and one must be wearing the Scapular at the moment of death.

A second great reward attached to the Scapular is the *Sabbatine,* enabling the Scapular wearer, by the fulfillment of two conditions in addition to wearing the Scapular, to *assure his liberation from Purgatory by the first Saturday after death.*

Three other rewards attached to the devotion are:

—A sharing in all the spiritual goods of the Carmelite order and of other Confraternity members throughout the world.

—More than one hundred plenary indulgences annually (upon fulfillment of conditions) and almost countless days of partial indulgences.

—Continual affiliation to Mary in a true devotion of perpetual homage, confidence and love.

The Scapular of Carmel must be made entirely of wool and, according to the Sacred Congregation of Indulgences (1868), the word "pannus" should be taken in its strict meaning, that is to say, as wool woven into cloth, and *not* wool worked with the needle after the fashion of lace, nor pressed (felt).

For the duration of the past world war, the Sacred Congregation permitted the use of other woven materials besides wool for brown Scapulars. Felt, knitted wear, lace, etc., were still invalid.

The color of the Scapular is usually dark drown, but may be any shade between brown and black.

The cords which join the two panels of the Scapular may be of any material and of any color.

Ornamentation of the Scapular is permitted (pictures of Our Lady are even customary), but the prescribed color of the Scapular must always predominate. If the Scapular bears a picture on each panel, the stitch securing the picture should be such that the Scapular obviously holds the picture and does not frame the picture so that the brown cloth would look more like a "backing" than the essential part of the garment. Lace borders on a picture-bearing Scapular definitely jeopardize its validity.

The Scapular must be rectangular in shape. Guard must be had against Scapulars either pinked or too much trimmed at the corners.

The Scapular must be worn over the shoulders in such a manner that one part hangs in front of the body and the other in the back. Worn in any other way, it carries no indulgences.

It is not necessary, however, to wear the Scapular next to the skin. It may be worn over one's clothes or even enclosed in some sort of case. In the latter event, the panels of the Scapular must be actually attached to the cords which should join them so that, were the covering removed, the Scapular would be intact."

For more information write to:

Carmelite National Shrine of Our Lady of the Scapular, The Scapular Apostolate, 338 E. 59th St., New York City, N. Y.

The Carmelite Fathers, who have a complete monopoly on this gold-mine devotion, claim a world-wide membership of two hundred millions—two hundred millions!

A Roman Catholic takes a new scapular at least once a year. It costs twenty cents, but many give one dollar and more.

Now you understand why the Carmelite Fathers agree with A. A. Lambing, D.D., L.D. who wrote, *"The Scapular of Our Lady has become one of the richest fountains of Grace which the Church, in her liberality, has opened to us."*

OUR LADY OF FATIMA

Here is another modern and very popular devotion to Mary for American Roman Catholics. I am reprinting a famous and official booklet of the Church of Rome—FATIMA AND YOU —which has the official imprimatur of Paul C. Schulte, D.D., Archbishop of Indianapolis, printed by Our Sunday Visitor Press, Huntington, Indiana.

"In the spring of 1916 three little shepherd children had one day taken their sheep to the pasture land near the Portuguese village of Fatima. It was just another "routine day" in the lives of Lucy, aged nine, her cousin, Francis, aged eight and his little sister, Jacinta, whose age was only six. "We had played only a short while," wrote Lucy many years later, "when a strong wind shook the trees and above them a light appeared, whiter than the driven snow. As it approached, it took the form of a young man, transparent with resplendent light. He began to speak: *'Fear not! I am the Angel of Peace. Pray with me.'* "

He knelt on the ground, bowed low and three times recited a prayer: *"My God, I believe, I adore, I hope and I love You. I beg pardon of You for those who do not believe, do not adore, do not hope and do not love You."* Then he arose and said: *"Pray this way. The hearts of Jesus and Mary are attentive to the voice of your supplications."*

Three times in all the Angel visited the children, the third time holding aloft a chalice with a host suspended above it, from which drops of blood fell into the chalice. Leaving both suspended in mid-air, he prostrated himself on the ground and three times recited this sublime prayer of reparation.

"Most Holy Trinity, Father, Son and Holy Ghost, I adore You profoundly and I offer You the most precious Body, Blood, Soul and Divinity of Jesus Christ, present in all the tabernacles of the world, in reparation for the outrages, sacrileges and indifferences by which He Himself is offended. And by the infinite merits of His Most Sacred Heart and the Immaculate Heart of Mary, I beg of You the conversion of poor sinners."

The Angel then arose, gave the host to Lucy and the contents of the chalice to Francis and Jacinta, saying:

"Take and drink the Body and Blood of Jesus Christ, horribly outraged by ungrateful men. Make reparation for their crimes and console your God."

Once more prostrating himself on the ground, he recited three times with the children the prayer *"Most Holy Trinity . . ."* Then he disappeared from view.

A year went by. On May 13th, 1917, in almost the same spot where the Angel had appeared, the children were once more tending their sheep. They had said their Rosary, finished their meagre luncheon and begun to play when suddenly, out of an azure blue sky, a brilliant flash of light appeared in the East. Fearing a storm, they were running excitedly to gather the sheep together and return home, when another flash, this time more brilliant than the first, literally rooted them to the spot. It had settled above the branches of a little holm oak tree and there, to their utter amazement, they beheld "the most beautiful Lady they had ever seen." *"It was,"* writes Lucy, *"a lady dressed all in white, more brilliant than the sun, shedding rays of light clearer and stronger than a crystal glass filled with the most sparkling water pierced by the burning rays of the sun."*

Six times in all, monthly from May till October, the beautiful Lady appeared to the children. Over and over she stressed the necessity of penance; told them that men must cease offending her Divine Son, already too grievously offended and urged them to "pray the Rosary . . . pray the Rosary" to bring to an end the war then raging and to ensure peace for the world.

During the July apparition the Mother of God showed those innocent children a terrifying vision of Hell. "She opened her hands and the light issuing from them seemed to penetrate into the very depths of the earth. Even the earth itself seemed to vanish and we saw huge numbers of devils and damned souls in a vast and fiery ocean. The devils resembled hideous black animals each filling the air with despairing shrieks. The damned souls were in their human bodies and seemed brown in color, tumbling about constantly in the flames screaming with terror. All were on fire within and without their bodies, and neither devils nor damned souls seemed able to control their movements. They were tossing about like fiery coals in a furnace, with never an instant's peace or freedom from pain." So terrible was the vision that Lucy said they would have died of fright were it not for the fact that the Mother of God was near and had told them that they themselves would go to Heaven. To the children she now explained:

"You have seen Hell, where the souls of poor sinners go. To save them, God wishes to establish throughout the world devotion to my Immaculate Heart. If people do what I tell you, many souls will be saved and there will be peace.

"But if they do not stop offending God, another and more terrible war will break out in the reign of Pius XI. When a night illumined by an unknown light is seen, know that this is the signal that God gives that the chastisement of the world for its many transgressions is at hand."

(The unknown light in question was seen all over Europe the night of January 25th, 1938. It was an ominous red glow, as if great cities were on fire. Three months later Hitler invaded Austria. The "chastisement of the world" was about to become a terrible reality, the *most* terrible reality mankind has ever known.)

"To prevent this" the Blessed Virgin continued, (N. B. to *prevent* the second World War, which *could* have been pre-

vented had people heeded the warnings of Mary at Fatima), *"I shall come to ask the consecration of Russia to my Immaculate Heart and the Communion of Reparation on the first Saturdays. If people heed my request, Russia will be converted and there will be peace. If not, she shall spread her errors throughout the world, promoting wars and persecution of the Church. The good will be martyred; the Holy Father will suffer much; different nations will be destroyed but in the end my Immaculate Heart will triumph. The Holy Father will consecrate Russia to me, which will be converted and some time of peace will be given to the world."*

During the July apparition the Blessed Virgin had told the children that in October she would work a miracle so great that all would believe her predictions and promises. Therefore it was to be expected that all roads would lead to Fatima on the days preceding this final apparition. O Dia, a secular newspaper of Lisbon, had this to say of the night of October 12th, 1917.

"All night long and into the early morning a light, persistent rain fell. It soaked the fields, saddened the air and chilled to the bone the men, women and children and the beasts plodding their way to the hill of the miracle. The rain kept falling, a soft, unending drizzle. Drops trickled down the women's skirts of coarse wool or striped cotton, making them weighty as lead. Water dripped from the caps and broad-brimmed hats of the men, onto the new jackets of their suits for seeing God. The bare feet of the women and the hob-nailed shoes of the men sloshed in the wide pools of the muddy roads. They seemed not to notice the rain."

Morning dawned. The ground was a veritable quagmire. Yet the light of day saw 70,000 people crowded together, singing hymns, praying the Rosary, undismayed by the dark lowering clouds and the relentless, never-ending rain. Among the vast throng were atheists and scoffers who welcomed the impending showdown, confident that the events of the day would give the lie to all those silly and stupid fairy tales about miracles and a Lady from Heaven. There were even ugly rumors of violent treatment of the children and their parents should the affair turn out to be a fiasco. But never was it more strikingly manifested that "those who came to scoff remained to pray."

Just at noon the familiar flash appeared towards the East. *"Silence, Our Lady is coming!"* cried Lucy. Her words were passed from person to person till the whole vast assembly grew tense and alert with excited expectancy. The faces of the children assumed an ecstatic expression and the people nearby realized that once more they were gazing at the Beautiful Lady from above. The interview was brief. The Lady kept the promise made in the first apparition to tell them who she was. She announced: *"I am the Lady of the Rosary."* Then her face grew very grave as she imparted her last message to the children:

"People must amend their lives, ask pardon for their sins and not offend Our Lord any more for He is already too much offended." As she took her leave of the children, she opened her hands and from them rays of light extended in the direction of the sun. *"There she goes, there she goes!"* shouted Lucy, and her words found echo in a great cry of astonishment from the multitudes, now observing the first awe-inspiring manifestations of the stupendous miracle of the sun.

Gradually the sun grew pale, lost its normal color and appeared as a sort of silver disc at which all could gaze directly without even shading their eyes. Then, to the astonishment of all present, rays of multi-colored light shot out from the sun in every direction; red, blue, green, yellow—every color of the spectrum. Meanwhile, the whole heavens seemed to be revolving as the sun spun madly on its axis like a gigantic wheel of fire, painting the rocks, the trees, the faces of the people with sunshine such as human eye had never seen before. Three times it stopped and three times the mad dance was resumed. Then while the crowd fell to its knees in sheer terror, the sun suddenly seemed to be torn loose from its place in the heavens. Down it hurtled, closer and closer to earth staggering "drunkenly" as it zigzagged through the skies while from all parts of the now thoroughly terrified multitude arose cries of repentance and appeals for mercy. *"It's the end of the world!"* shrieked one woman hysterically. *"Dear God, don't let me die in my sins!"* cried another. *"Holy Virgin, protect us!"* implored a third. But just when it seemed that the end was at hand, the sun suddenly resumed its accustomed place in the heavens, whence it shone forth as peacefully as before.

Meanwhile, the children alone were privileged to witness a Heavenly Tableau "at the side of the sun." Our Lady re-appeared, first with St. Joseph and the Divine Infant, then with her Divine Son as a grown Man, blessing the assembled crowd and finally in the garb of Our Lady of Mount Carmel.

Thus the stupendous miracle of the sun, the stamp of Divine approval on the promises made to humankind by God's own Blessed Mother. For this is the age of Mary. If our world is to be saved it will be saved through Mary and since Almighty God has placed the peace of the world in her hands she has done all in her power to give that peace to a weary and despairing world. But that peace will not be ours without our own co-operation. That she has made abundantly clear. The Mother of God needs, pleads for your help and mine. In this pilgrimage she is literally "hurrying around the world" in search of that "sufficient number" who will hear her requests and help her hold back the avenging hand of Her Divine Son from descending in punishment on a heedless and sinful world. This may, indeed, be the last call for peace on earth in our generation; last loving appeal of a mother's heart to a world that has turned back on God, her Son. If it be heard, Russia will be converted and there will be peace. If not, the errors of Communism will spread *throughout the entire world* and the Mother of God *did not exclude the United States of America.*

The Pilgrim Virgin Statue

America's "pilgrim Virgin" is one of two images of Our Lady of Fatima blessed for similar pilgrimages by the Bishop of Fatima in 1947 at the famous Portuguese shrine. Both are hand-carved from cedarwood by Thedim, famed Portuguese sculptor, who designed the original now in the Fatima basilica. The first statue was blessed on May 13th, 1947 and is now touring Europe; the second on October 13th, 1947, anniversary of Our Lady's final apparition at Fatima, in the presence of 200,000 pilgrims. Immediately after the blessing America's Pilgrim Virgin was flown to the United States and taken by automobile to Ottawa, Canada. There it was crowned by the Archbishop, Most Rev. Alexandre Vachon, D.D., preparatory to starting its long journey through Canada and the United States. Since then it has visited many Dioceses in the East, Midwest and South and more than two million people have venerated the famed image.

The purpose of this pilgrimage is to invite millions of people to join in a Crusade of prayer and reparation for world peace and the conversion of Russia, as promised by Our Blessed Mother at Fatima in 1917. The pilgrimage is under the direction of Most Rev. John F. O'Hara, D.D., Bishop of Buffalo."—From: "Fatima and you."

COMMENT

That vision at Fatima would need a terrific quantity of explaining on the part of someone in order to deceive an intelligent person. How the sun could leave its place in the heavens, and plunge and zig-zag upon the crowd, only stopping and returning to its place when a collision with the earth seemed inevitable, seems too fantastic to be true. I do know that under certain conditions there are those who see pink elephants, purple alligators, or a host of beetles.

Now let us consider some facts and figures. The earth is not quite 8,000 miles in diameter, while that of the sun is about 860,000 miles. The distance of the sun from the earth varies between $94\frac{1}{2}$ million and $91\frac{1}{2}$ million miles. The sun evolves an intense heat, which is of several thousand degrees centigrade —more than enough to scorch the witnesses of the vision to a cinder and vaporize the cinder.

Mercury, the nearest planet to the sun, a distance of approximately 37 million miles, has a surface temperature of 350 degrees centigrade, which is enough to melt lead. Therefore, we can see what would happen to our own planet if the sun came near enough to it, with its surface temperature of 6,000 degrees centigrade.

Did you ever really thank God for being a Christian and not a Roman Catholic, and for the privilege you have to read and follow the beautiful and simple Word of God, which gives you light to discern the errors and inventions of a man-made church? Thank God now with all your heart.

CHAPTER SEVEN

Answers to Questions on Catholic Doctrines *

(*All texts of Scripture are from the official Roman Catholic version of the Bible.*)

THE CHURCH

Are all true Believers "catholic" or "universal"?

Yes, because they do not localize themselves in space, time or denomination, but they follow the Bible teaching that the catholic church of Christ consists of all Christians who have truly received Christ as Personal Saviour and have been born from above (John 3:3) regardless of denomination. (Matt. 18:20, Col. 1:18, I Cor. 12:13.)

What do Roman Catholics mean by the word "church"?

In the Roman Catholic Baltimore Catechism, question 115, we read: "Q. What is the Church? A. The Church is the congregation of all those who profess the faith of Christ, and are governed by their lawful pastors under one visible head (the pope)."

The Roman church applies exclusively to itself the term "catholic or universal." Has it any right to this claim?

No, because it is localized and limited, its seat is in Rome and it teaches that only those who "are governed by its lawful pastors under one visible head" (the pope) are its members.

*Reprinted from my copyrighted pamphlet, "Pocket Question Box."

PETER

Is the text of the Rock a proof of Peter's supremacy?

No. Jesus did not say to Peter, upon thee I will build my church, as the church of Rome claims, but, "upon this rock," and the word "this" pointing to Himself, whom Peter had confessed when he said, "Thou art Christ," as it can be seen from the Greek where two words are used: "Petros" and "Petra" (Matt. 16:18).

Do the Scriptures clearly say that Christ is the rock?

Yes. "And that rock was Christ" I Cor. 10:4 (see also I Cor. 3:11, I Peter 2:6).

Do the Scriptures confirm the Roman teaching that Peter was the head of the Apostles?

No. All the apostles were equal. (Matt. 23:10, 11). At the Council of Jerusalem Peter took part in the disputations, but the apostle James, and not Peter, presided and pronounced the Council's decision. (Acts 15:13, 19.) Peter calls himself an elder and never Chief Apostle. (I Peter 5:1.)

Did the other Apostles recognize Peter as their chief?

No. In fact they sent Peter forth to preach, rather than Peter sending them. (Acts 8:14.) Paul declared that he was "behind the very chiefest apostle in nothing (II Cor. 12:11, 12), and withstood Peter to the face (Gal. 2:11), and claimed authority over the Roman Church itself (Rom. 1:5, 6; 16:17). He maintained that whatever Peter was to the Jews he, Paul, was to the Gentiles (Gal. 7:7, 8). As James D. Bales says in the booklet "Was Peter Pope?": "If Peter was the chief it was the duty of Paul and of the Apostles to recognize him and respect him as such and to teach such a fundamental doctrine but neither the Gospels nor the Acts of the Apostles, the Epistles nor Revelation mention it."

TRADITION

What is the rule of faith of the Church of Rome?
Scripture and Tradition.

What does the Roman Catholic Church mean by Tradition?

The decrees of the popes and of the Councils, the contents of which, they say, Christ and His Apostles taught by word of mouth, but which were not written down in the Bible.

Can the Church of Rome prove that its tradition is divine or apostolic?

No. If the Roman Church could prove that its Tradition were divine or apostolic we would bow at once to its authority. Tradition at first was oral, but who can be trusted to report? The Fathers or the Councils? They contradict one another and even the present Roman teaching on many points.

Is there any remarkable instance in the Bible, in which report or tradition circulated a falsehood?

Yes. In John 21:22, 23, we read *"Jesus said to him, 'If I wish him to remain until I come, what is that to thee? Do thou follow me.' This saying therefore went abroad among the brethren, that that disciple was not to die. But Jesus had not said to him; 'He is not to die'; but rather, 'If I wish him to remain until I come, what is that to thee'?"* Surely we can not depend for our salvation on oral report.

Does John 21:25 prove that God's revelation is also contained in Tradition?

> *"There are however many other things that Jesus did but if every one of these should be written, etc."*

No. While it must be admitted that Jesus and his Apostles said and did many things that are not written in the Bible, the important fact is that the Scriptures were indited by the Holy

Spirit and are sufficient for our every need. St. John himself, in the preceding chapter quoted above, declares:

"But these are written that you may believe that Jesus is the Christ, the Son of God, and that believing you may have life in his name." John 20:31.

Does the following passage of St. Paul justify the claims of Tradition?

"So then, brethren, stand firm, and hold the teachings that you have learned, whether by word or by letters of ours." II Thess. 2:15.

No. We do not deny that what is contained in the New Testament was first taught by word of mouth; but we know the Holy Spirit saw to it that everything necessary was later written down in the Bible. There is nothing in the above quotation of St. Paul to support the claims of Tradition.

How do you answer Roman Catholics when they quote in favor of Tradition the following text?

"I had much to write to thee, but I do not want to write to thee with pen and ink. But I hope to see thee shortly, and we will speak face to face." III John 13:14.

The Bible does not undertake to set forth in detail all the exhortations and disciplinary counsels uttered by Jesus Christ and His Apostles; it does, however, give all that is necessary for our salvation, growth and guidance in grace.

Did Christ condemn Tradition?

Yes.

"So you have made void the commandment of God by your tradition." Matt. 15:7.

Does St. Paul warn us against Tradition?

Yes.

"Beware lest any man cheat you by philosophy, and vain deceit; according to the tradition of men, according to the elements of the world, and not according to Christ." Col. 2:8.

What is the rule of faith of Believers?

The Holy Scriptures, and only the Holy Scriptures.

How shall we answer Roman Catholics when they claim that the Scriptures are not the only rule of faith because the Apostles were not commanded to write but to preach?

The Holy Spirit did more than command, for He actually inspired the disciples to write.

Did Christ appeal to the Scriptures as the rule of faith?

Yes, and many times. He resisted Satan with Scripture. (Matt. 4:4). He said that the Sadducees erred because they did not know the Scripture (Matt. 22:29). He reproved the two disciples as they journeyed to Emmaus because they did not believe all that the Prophets said of Him (Luke 24:25, 27). He quoted the Scriptures very often (Luke 16:31—John 5:39, etc.).

Did the Apostles appeal to the Scriptures?

Yes. The Apostles followed the example of their Master in often quoting the Scriptures. (See Acts 17:2, 18:24, 26:22, II Tim. 3:15.)

Did Christ and the Apostles ever appeal to Tradition?

No, not even once.

How can you prove that the Christians, in the Apostles' time, had the same rule of faith as ourselves?

They had the Old Testament, and the teaching of Christ and

His Apostles. We have the Old Testament and the New Testament which is the teaching of Christ and His Apostles.

PURGATORY

What is purgatory according to the Roman Church?

"Purgatory is the state in which those suffer for a time who die guilty of venial sins, or without having satisfied for the punishment due to their sins." Baltimore Catechism.

Upon what doctrine is purgatory founded?

Purgatory is founded upon the Roman inventions of venial sin, and temporal punishment of sin after death.

Is there such a thing as venial sin?

No. One sin may be more heinous than the other (Jer. 7:26 - John 19:11); but *"the wages of sin is death"* (Rom. 6:23). The Apostle does not speak of just some sins, but of all sins. The Bible never makes distinction between mortal and venial sin. (See also Gal. 3:10- James 2:10.)

What does the Roman Catholic mean by temporal punishment due to sin?

According to Roman teaching, two kinds of punishment are due to mortal sin: eternal (in hell forever), and temporal (in purgatory). Eternal punishment is cancelled by the sacraments of Baptism and Extreme Unction, or by an act of perfect contrition with promise of confession. *Temporal punishment,* they teach, is not cancelled by these sacraments, but *by works of penance, by almsgiving, by paying a priest to say a Mass, etc.,* which reduce the temporal punishment for mortal sins that would have to be suffered in Purgatory.

Is purgatory a place for bad Roman Catholics or for good and saintly ones?

According to the Roman teaching even the greatest saints may have to pass through the fires of purgatory.

Is the doctrine of satisfaction for temporal punishment scriptural?

No. According to the Bible teaching no one has to satisfy for the punishment due to his sin, since Jesus Christ, Our Saviour, has satisfied for us freely and completely by His sacrifice on the cross. Our faith in Jesus Christ alone obtains forgiveness for us, not our works. (Eph. 2:8, 9 - Rom. 3:24 - Heb. 10:14 - Rom. 8:1 - Col. 2:13.)

Is purgatory ever mentioned in the Bible?

No. Some teach that there was a place apart from hell and heaven where Christ went after his crucifixion, and where the believers of the Old Testament were waiting for the Saviour. But this view should not be confused with the Roman purgatory, which Roman Catholics believe to be a place where believers are tortured for an indefinite period of time in expiation of their sins.

Why is the Roman teaching of purgatory fundamentally opposed to Christian teaching?

Because it casts dishonor upon the redeeming work of the Incarnate Son of God. Purgatory takes away from the fullness of Christ's love for his church, and is a denial of the completeness and sufficiency of His sacrifice and mediatorial work.

Have you any other reason for rejecting purgatory?

Yes. We reject it because the Scriptures say that the believer after death enters into rest; returns to God, and that no brother can redeem.

"Blessed are the dead who die in the Lord. From hence-forth now, saith the Spirit, that they may rest from their labours" Rev. (Apoc.) 14:13 (Eccl. 12:7; Luke 16:22; Philip 1:23).

"No brother can redeem, nor shall man redeem: he shall not give God his ransom, nor the price of the redemption of his soul" Ps. 48:7, 8 (II Tim. 2:12; Acts 10:43).

THE SACRIFICE OF
THE MASS

What is the main office of Roman priests?

To sacrifice the real body, blood, soul, and deity of Christ, i.e., to celebrate the Mass.

What do Roman Catholics mean by the Mass?

The Council of Trent, Sess. 22, chapts. 1, 3, Can. 1, 2, 3, says:

1—*"There is in the (Roman) Catholic Church a true sacrifice, the mass, instituted by Jesus Christ; it is the sacrifice of the body and blood of Christ under the appearances of bread and wine."*

2—*"This sacrifice is identical with the sacrifice of the Cross, inasmuch as Jesus Christ is priest and victim both. The only difference lies in the manner of offering, which is bloody upon the Cross and bloodless on our altars.*

3—*It is a propitiatory sacrifice, atoning for our sins, and the sins of the living and of the dead in Christ, for whom it is offered."*

Did Christ command His Apostles to offer the sacrifice of the Mass?

No. He commanded them to preach the Gospel, but He did not mention the sacrifice of the Mass, which is considered by Rome the main duty of its priests.

The following texts of the Bible are quoted in favor of the sacrifice of the Roman Catholic mass: Malachi, they say, foretold the abolition of the Mosaic sacrifices, and the establishing of the sacrifice of the mass, which was to be offered up everywhere.

"I have no pleasure in you (the Jewish priests), saith the Lord of Hosts, neither will I accept an offering at your hand. For, from the rising of the sun, even unto the going down of the same, My name shall be great among the Gentiles; and in every place incense shall be offered unto My name and a pure offering" (Malachi 1:10, 11).

Christ commanded the Apostles, and through them all the bishops and priests of the Catholic church, to repeat often that sacrifice (the mass): *"Do this in remembrance of Me"* (Luke 22:19).

The Acts of the Apostles give us an account of the worship of the early Christians. Is there any allusion to the sacrifice of the Mass?

No. We read of prayers, praise, the administration of Baptism, the Lord's Supper, the preaching of the Gospel, but nothing about the sacrifice of the Mass.

St. Paul gives many exhortations to Timothy and Titus for the government of their churches, and their duties. Does he mention the sacrifice or celebration of the Mass as their duty?

No. He speaks of prayers and preaching of the Gospel and other duties, but not even one word about the sacrifice of the Mass.

Do we need any "sacrificing priests" under the Gospel dispensation?

No. Christ is the only High Priest and every believer is a priest to offer up spiritual sacrifices acceptable to God by Jesus Christ. (I Peter 2:5)

Can you give me any scriptural proofs why we do not need any "sacrificing priests"?

Yes. The Bible gives three reasons for the abolition of the Jewish priesthood, and these reasons apply with equal force to the Roman priesthood.

The Jewish priesthood was unprofitable:

1—*Because they were many;*
2—*Because they needed to offer up sacrifices for their own sins;*
3—*Because they were men of infirmity.* Heb. 7:23, 28.

Was not the sacrifice of Jesus on the Cross all-sufficient?

Yes. The Bible says: *"For by one offering He has perfected FOREVER those who are sanctified"* Heb. 10:14. *"We have been sanctified through the offering of the body of Jesus Christ Once For All" Heb.* 10:10.

Do the Scriptures definitely declare that there is only one sacrifice?

Yes. *"He does not need to offer sacrifice daily (as the other priests did) first for his own sins and then for the sins of the people, for this latter He did Once For All in offering up Himself"* Heb 7:27.

"And just as it is appointed unto men to die once, but after that comes the judgment, so also was Christ offered ONCE to take away the sins of many" (Heb. 9:27, 28).

Did Malachi (1:10, 11) foretell the abolition of the Mosaic sacrifices, and the establishing of the sacrifice of the Mass, which was to be offered up everywhere?

In the Bible, prayers, praise, obedience, a contrite spirit and heart, are represented as incense, and oblation or sacrifice.

"Let my prayer be set forth before Thee as incense, and the lifting up of my hands as the evening sacrifice" (Psalm 141:2).

"Let us offer up a sacrifice of praise always to God, that is, fruit of lips praising His name" (Heb. 13:15).

These are the pure sacrifices foretold by Malachi, because though imperfect in themselves, they are pure as presented by our High Priest, Christ.

"For in Him dwells all the fullness of the Godhead bodily, and in Him who is the head of every principality and power, you have received of that fullness" (Col. 2:10).

Therefore there is no prophecy about the mass in Malachi's words.

Is Christ a priest according to the order of Melchisedec on account of the sacrifice of the Mass, prefigured by the bread and wine offered by Melchisedec? (Gen. 14:18)

No. Melchisedec brought bread and wine to refresh Abraham and his followers, not to sacrifice. The Roman version is a mistranslation. It translates *"And* he was a priest," as follows: *"For* he was a priest," in order to make it appear that he brought forth bread and wine in his official capacity as a priest to offer sacrifice with them.

The Psalmist says, *"Thou art a priest forever, according to the order of Melchisedec"* (Psalm 110:4). Christ is a priest according to the order of Melchisedec on account of the sacrifice of the mass, prefigured by the bread and wine offered by Melchisedec: *"And Melchisedec, King of Salem, brought forth bread and wine, for he was the priest of the Most High God"* (Gen. 14:18).

It is significant that St. Paul, describing the character and conduct of Melchisedec (Heb. 7), says nothing about Melchisedec offering bread and wine as a type of the sacrifice of the Roman Catholic mass.

The power of celebrating mass is the chief pretense of the Roman priesthood, but there is not one word about this sacrifice in the New Testament. Christ sent the Apostles *to preach and baptize and not to say mass:*

"*Go, therefore and make disciples of all nations, baptizing them in the name, etc.*" (Matt. 28:19).

Do priests charge for masses?

Yes. They charge $1.00, $5.00, $35.00, $100.00 or more according to the kind of mass the Roman Catholic desires; *and this is the sin of Simon Magus* (Acts 8:18, 24).

Do Roman Catholics understand the priests when they say Mass?

No, unless they use a translation. The priests say the Mass in Latin, a language the people do not understand. The Scriptures say: "*Yet in the church, I had rather speak five words with my understanding, that by my voice I might teach others also, than ten thousand words in an unknown tongue*" I Cor. 14: 19.

Is the Roman Mass adopted from paganism?

Yes. The daily sacrifice of the Mass is copied from the victim—hostia—of the heathen ritual. *The roundness of the wafer* used in the mass is taken from Egyptian mythology—*a round disk symbolizing Osiris, the sun Divinity.*—The letters on the wafer I.H.S. (*Jesus Hominum Salvator*—"*Jesus the Saviour of men*") are taken from the Roman and Egyptian trinity *Isis, Horus, Seb (the Mother, the Child, and the Father of the Gods).*

MARY and SAINTS

Does the following text of Gen. 3:15, prove the Roman teaching of the Immaculate Conception of Mary?

"She shall crush thy head, and thou shalt lie in wait for her heel."

No. The Hebrew text reads "He" or "It," not SHE (Mary) shall crush, etc., and even the Septuagint version, approved by the Roman Catholic church reads "He shall crush," etc. Therefore the subtle argumentation from the above text in favor of the dogma of the Immaculate Conception has no scriptural foundation.

Does Luke 1:28, prove the Roman doctrine of the Immaculate Conception?

"Hail, full of Grace, the Lord is with thee, blessed art thou amongst women."

No. The Angel saluted Mary with a gracious benediction on the ground that she was chosen from among all other women to become the mother of Jesus. But the Angel did not say or imply that she was conceived without original sin, or that she did not need salvation. Mary knew herself to be a sinner and in need of salvation, for in her song of praise she said: "And my spirit hath rejoiced in God my Saviour." Luke 1:47. The Immaculate Conception was defined as dogma on Dec. 8, 1854, against the teachings of many theologians—Augustine, Cardinal Cajetan, St. Thomas Aquinas, and Pope Gregory the Great, etc. It is clear teaching of the Scriptures that *all* die in Adam (Cf. I Cor. 15:22; Rom. 5:12; Ps. 14:3; Rom. 3:23; Isaiah 64:6).

In the Bible the brethren are often asked to pray for others. Does this prove the Roman teaching of prayers to the Saints? (James 5:16, 18; Gen. 20:7; Rom. 15:30)

No. The above passages of the Bible do not prove that a living Christian should pray to a dead saint to intercede for him, but only that Christians, while on earth, should pray for each other. In heaven none can mediate but Christ. (I Tim. 2:5)

Does Luke 16:27 prove that we can pray to the Saints?

> *"And he said, then, father, I beseech thee to send him to my father's house,"* etc.

No. The conduct of a lost soul (the rich man) is not proper example for Christians. Besides, his prayers were of no effect. The texts do not prove the Roman doctrine of prayers to dead saints by living persons.

Does the Bible forbid prayers to dead saints?

Yes. (Col. 2:18; Acts 14:14; Matt. 6:6) Christ is our only mediator. (Acts 4:12; Rom. 8:34; Rev. 22:9.)

Can Roman Catholics explain how dead saints can hear our prayers?

No. Some Roman Catholics say that the saints acquire the knowledge of our prayers from the angels. But how do the angels acquire their knowledge? Others say that the saints see all things in God. But if they see all things in God they have the same knowledge as God and therefore are as omniscient as God. Others think that prayers offered to dead saints are communicated to them by God. But then the saints, who are supposed to mediate for us before God, would have their knowledge of our prayers from the same person with whom they are supposed to intercede.

INTENTION and SACRAMENTS

Roman Catholics claim that grace and salvation are given through

the sacraments, but are they certain of validly receiving the sacraments?

No, because the validity of the sacraments depends upon the intention of the priest. The Council of Trent (Sess. VII. Can. 11) declares: "If anyone shall say, that intention, at least of doing what the church does, is not required in ministers while performing and administering the sacraments, let him be anathema." Cardinal Bellarmine, who is considered a doctor of the Roman Church, admits that: "No one can be certain, with the certainty of faith, that he has received a true sacrament, since no sacrament is performed without the intention of the ministers, and no one can see the intention of another"—Bellarmine's Works, Vol. I, p. 488.

Are Roman Catholics certain of being Christian, and not pagan?

No. According to the Baltimore Catechism (Q. 152, 153), for instance, "Baptism is a sacrament which cleanses us from original sin, makes us children of God and heirs of heaven." "Baptism is necessary to salvation, because without it we cannot enter the kingdom of heaven." But if the priest or the person who baptizes a child is lacking in the proper "intention," the child can never enter heaven. But Cardinal (Saint) Bellarmine assures us that "no one can see the intention of another," and thus, even though the rite of baptism is properly performed on a child, it will have no effect if the proper "intention" is lacking in the person who performs the rite.

Are Roman Catholics certain that their priest, bishop, pope are validly ordained, and not still pagan?

No. Suppose a child is baptized by a priest who lacks the proper intention. The baptism is then of no avail, and the child grows up a pagan. If he should enter a seminary and be ordained a priest, his ordination will be also invalid. All the thousands of masses he says, all the sacraments he performs, will likewise be invalid. If he becomes a bishop, the priests he ordains and the other bishops he consecrates will have no power as such. If by chance he should become Pope, the Roman Catholic church would then have as "Vicar of Christ," and "infallible head" a man who was not even a Christian to start with.

CONFESSION

According to the Bible, who can forgive sin?
Only the Godhead. (Ps. 54:4; Is. 33:22; Mich. 7:18; Mark 2:7, 10.)

According to the Roman church, who can forgive sins?
The priests. The Roman church teaches that Christ has established on earth a tribunal, or court of justice, where its priests sit as judges and forgive sinners who confess them.

Does not the power of "binding and loosing" (Matt. 18:18) and of remitting and retaining (John 20:23) give to the priest authority for remitting sins in confession?

No. Christ gave the power of binding or loosing, remitting or retaining to the Apostles and not to the priests. The Apostles never claimed the power of forgiving sins by absolution as the Roman priests do, but only by the preaching of salvation through Jesus Christ, who bore our guilt, paid our debt, and set us free from condemnation forever (I John 1:7; Rom. 8:1, I Peter 2:24).

MATRIMONY

Does Paul (Eph. 5:25, 32) teach that marriage is a sacrament instituted by Christ?

No. Matrimony was instituted by God in Paradise, thousands of years before Christ, and therefore it is not an institution of the new law. Paul does not say that matrimony is a sacrament but "this is a great mystery."

Does the Roman church recognize divorce?

Theoretically, the Roman church does not recognize divorce, but practically allows divorce by its system of annulment and dispensation, especially for rich and influential people, as, for example, for Lucrezia Borgia and Giovanni Sforza in 1497; Louis XII and Jeanne of Valois, in 1498; Henry IV and Marguerite de Valois; the Duke of Marlborough and Miss Vanderbilt; Marconi and Miss O'Brien, etc., etc.

Is marriage between a baptized Protestant and an infidel, or unbaptized Protestant, considered valid by the church of Rome?

Before May 19, 1918, such a marriage was invalid. After that date it is considered valid.

Does the Roman church consider valid a marriage of a Catholic performed by a Protestant minister or a Justice of the Peace?

Before April 19, 1908, such a marriage was valid; after that date it is considered invalid.

Is the non-Roman Catholic party marrying a Roman Catholic obliged to keep the promise to baptize and educate the children in the Roman Catholic Church?

It may bind as a civil contract, but no promise, even if signed in the presence of a priest, can, in the eyes God, compel parents to sign over their unborn children to a religion whose doctrines are against the Bible teachings.

IMAGES

Does the command of God to make the cherubims (Exodus 25:18, 19) prove the Roman teaching of veneration of images?

No. The cherubims were not adored or venerated, nor were they even seen by the people. They were in the Holy of Holies into which the High Priest alone entered once a year, and then only with the blood of a sacrifice. The cherubims were made at the express command of God, while the Church of Rome can not produce one such command enjoining the use and making of images.

Does the brazen serpent (Num. 21:9) prove the Roman veneration of images?

No. The brazen serpent is rather a proof against the worship of images. In fact, King Hezekiah later broke the serpent when the people burned incense before it (II Kings 18:4), as Roman Catholics do today before their images.

Do the Old and New Testaments forbid the use of images?
Yes. (Exodus 20:4, 5; Lev. 26:1; John 4:24; Acts 17:25; I Cor. 10:20.)

Do Roman Catholics try to justify the use of images by making a distinction in their worship?

Yes. They make a distinction between the cult of Latria, given only to the Godhead; the cult of hyper-dulia, given only to Mary; and the cult of dulia, given to the Saints, images and relics, but this distinction is only theoretical.

INDULGENCES

What do Roman Catholics mean by indulgences?

"It is a remission of the whole or part of the temporal punishment due to forgiven sin, granted by the Pope and the Bishops out of the Church's spiritual treasury, which is made up of the infinite redemptive merits of Jesus Christ, and the superabundant merits of the saints. It is more than the mere remission of canonical works of penance, for it really remits the whole or part of the punishment due the sinner by God, either here or in Purgatory." Roman Question Box, by Conway.

Why do true believers reject the Roman teaching of indulgences?

Because they do not need a pope or a bishop to grant them the merits of Christ as a reward for works of penance, money, wearing of scapular, etc., since they are justified, not by works, but by faith. (Gal. 2:16; Rom. 5:1.)

No saints, or any other Christian, are able to gain superabundant merits of works to be applied to us, or the souls in purgatory, because they cannot gain merit even for themselves, since we are all sinners and "all our righteousnesses are as filthy rags." Isaiah 64:6. "Even so you also, when you have done everything that was commanded you, say, 'We are unprofitable servants; we have done what was our duty to do' " Luke 17:10.

CHAPTER EIGHT

Should Protestants Marry Catholics

A Protestant cannot marry a Roman Catholic unless he or she goes to a priest for instruction.

A Roman Catholic should not be allowed to marry a Protestant unless he or she goes to a minister for instruction.

Several ministers are following my suggestion: as soon as they know about a probable mixed marriage they invite personally the Roman Catholic party for a period of lessons on the Bible. See the previous chapter which could be used for instructions for a mixed marriage. All texts of Scriptures are from the official Roman Catholic version of the Bible.

A Roman Catholic marrying a Protestant, and a Protestant marrying a Roman Catholic go against the wishes and counsels of their churches.

There seems to be only one possible and logical solution if the couple want to get married: both to accept the same faith, the same religion, and therefore there will be no need of a mixed marriage.

Which one should give up his faith, the Protestant party or the Roman Catholic? This is my advice if you are contemplating a mixed marriage.

Both the Roman church and the Protestant church claim to follow the teachings of the Bible, then the teachings of the Bible should decide which religion is false and to be repudiated, and which religion is true and to be accepted.

This is a fair proposition and if one of you will refuse for personal or family reasons, then I doubt that there is sufficient understanding and love to justify your marriage at all.

You will be responsible to God, not for what your minister, your priest, your families and friends believe and tell you, but for what your conscience, enlightened by the Scripture and the Holy Spirit tells you is good or evil. God gave you enough intelligence to understand the Scriptures because if they cannot be understood by the people, they were written in vain. Religion is true, not because you are born into a family which believes in it, nor because someone else claims that it is the only true religion; but the Bible, which is the Word of God to men, is the rule by which different churches are judged. "Prove all things; hold fast that which is good" (I Thess. 5:21). "Beloved, believe not every spirit, but try the spirits whether they are of God; because many false prophets have gone forth into the world" (I John 4:1).

The Scriptures do not ask you to learn the truth from this or that man, but they appeal directly to you; you have the capacity of discovering which is truth and which is error, if you take the Bible as your guide.

Accept that faith which you find to be true after prayer and Bible study, even if it means breaking with your friends, your relatives, or with your parents. The Lord Jesus Christ will be your friend and will guide you through a happy married life.

PRAYER! God, Almighty and eternal, Father of mericies,

I beseech thee, through the merits of that precious blood which was shed for us sinners by Thine only Son, Jesus Christ, our Lord and Saviour, to enlighten my mind and touch my heart, that I may follow the religion which Thou shalt reveal to me to be true, and abandon at whatever cost, that wherein I shall have discovered error and falsehood through the study of Thy Word, as revealed in the Holy Bible, for Jesus' sake, Amen.

Roman Catholic Demands for Mixed Marriages

(Extract from a Roman Catholic pamphlet, "Mixed Marriages," by Rev. G. Bampfield—International Catholic Truth Society, Brooklyn, N. Y.)

"THE CATHOLIC CHURCH does not like her children to marry those who are not Catholics. . . . Nor will she allow these marriages to take place at all until a solemn promise has been made by the two persons, the Protestant as well as the Catholic: First, that the Catholic, whether man or woman, shall have the fullest and freest use of the Catholic religion, and shall in no way be hindered from practicing it by the Protestant; secondly, that all the children of both sexes shall be baptized by a Catholic Priest, taken to the Catholic Church, sent to the Catholic school, and in every way taught and trained in the Catholic faith; thirdly, that the Catholic shall never cease praying and using all other wise and lawful means for the conversion of the Protestant.

To Protestants, perhaps to some Catholics, this may seem hard and stern. At all events, some will say, when all these promises have been made, surely then the Church will not dislike the marriage any longer. What can we want more than the free use of our religion and the bringing up of our children in the Faith?

Let us think about the matter . . . and take the very best case possible. Let us suppose that the husband you have married turns out really to be the good honest fellow he seemed to be before marriage; that he never bullies you about religion; does not even go on "nagging" at you about holy water and such "rubbish"; never hides away your scapular, or plays tricks with your beads, or pokes fun at dear old Father Doherty, your priest; does not growl at you for giving your big boy bread and cheese for his Friday's dinner; that he really leaves you alone, and lets you do what you like with the children; in fact that he is quite a treasure of a husband, barring his Protestantism; let us suppose all this, and even then is a mixed marriage a harmless thing or is it still that terrible evil of which the Church is so much afraid?

For most people it is fearfully hard to be good alone, when there is no one to believe and to live as they believe and live. Now, what is it you do in a mixed marriage? You positively take for your society, for your every-day and every-hour society, close into your own home and into the secrets of your heart, to have power and influence over you, to be part of you and one with you —you take one who, as he does not know the truth, cannot by any possibility help you to keep the truth or to do it. Nay! His desire ought to be, if he believes his own religion, to draw you away from what he thinks is error, though you know it to be the one road to Heaven. So you live your life, of your own accord, with this temptation. The more you love him, the greater the temptation. . . .

He promised not to prevent you going without meat on a Friday, but he never promised to go without it himself. He does not interfere with you; if he does look curiously and with just a twitch of a smile at your dry bread and cold herring, he says nothing to you; but for his own part he is not fond of fish, and he didn't marry you to live on dry bread; and as for such a lot of it in Lent and Ember days, and getting Jubilees and things, he can't make it all out: he is a horse that can't work without his corn, and good butcher's meat is the corn for him. Now, cooked meat smells as nice upon Fridays and Fast days—a trifle nicer, fancy—as it does upon other days. Then it is such a trouble, one dinner for husband, and another dinner for wife and children, and there are no fish to be had, and the eggs are so dear and so bad, and so, without a word from the Protestant husband, though he keeps his promise faithfully, the Catholic wife sees that butcher's meat upon Fast days is 'good for food, and pleasing to the eye,' and she takes and eats. . . .

When you marry a Protestant, you not only live with a temptation all your life, but your children live with a still stronger temptation; and the better the father is, and the more they do their duty of loving him, the stronger is the temptation that they feel. . . . To sit on his father's knee by the fireside, resting his curly head on that broad chest, to hold his hand for the summer stroll along the river bank, this was what your son loved. It was hard for him to think that the father who was so kind, and who gave him so many things, and who was so seldom cross to him, was all wrong about religion. He didn't see much difference between him and mother; of the two, perhaps, mother was the meanest, particularly, somehow, on Confession days. . . . The boy wonders and doubts instead of believing, and he is trained in the habit of doubt instead of the habit of faith. . . .

You see, I have dealt with you quite fairly. I have neither croaked nor made the worst of it, I have drawn you no pictures of drunken hands breaking the broomstick over you for going to Mass, and taking your boys to the Salvationist meeting just to tease you. I have supposed the best or nearly so. I will end by supposing the very, very best—the rarely best; the best so rarely that you dare not count upon it, or think that it will be in your own case, if you put aside the Church's counsel. I will suppose that your husband has not made you even cool about the Faith, and that your children are growing up first-rate Catholics, and yet, for all that, I say that you had far better have given him up, and let him marry that odious, red-haired Protestant creature, who tried so hard to get him. I will tell you why.

If, when you married a Protestant husband you gave up all idea of getting help from him on your road to Heaven, you could not give up your duty of helping him there. Before you married you promised, what would have been your duty whether you promised or not, that you would do your best in every lawful way to win him to the Faith. Getting your husband to Heaven is the one great duty of a wife. . . . But a year passed on, and another year, and still another, and yet . . . he was very far from being a Catholic. Your hands grew heavy with being lifted up in prayers, and your heart grew sad because you had been praying so long in vain. You knew that your marriage had taken from him every excuse of ignorance. If ever a man had a chance of knowing the Catholic Faith, it was he; if ever a man had a road into the Church made easy by natural helps, it was he; no excuse for him not being near the Faith, no excuse of having to leave wife or child. Knowing, that you were taught, that through the Catholic Church lies the road to Heaven, the thought that he was not on that road, hung upon you day by day like a weight of lead. For all he was so tender and so good, for all you loved him so much and were so near his heart, between you and him lay a cloud—a division—a want of something that should have made you one. . . .

So your life is weighed down with care. Between you and the heart which should be wholly one with you is fixed the greatest gulf that can divide man from man, difference of worship and Faith; in your highest feelings he has no interest, the things which are dearest to you are follies to him and he puts them by with a smile; besides this separation, there is the unending heartache of seeing him standing on a precipice from which you cannot snatch him. There is also the chance of watching a death-bed to which you can bring no help, and of burying him in a grave by the side of which you stand mourning with a desperate hopefulness which is but the shadow of true hope. Is this a happy married life?"

Why the non-Catholic Church opposes Roman Catholic Demands for Mixed Marriages

(Extracts from a Christian pamphlet, "If I marry a Roman Catholic," by Leland Foster Wood, 297 Fourth Ave., New York 10, N. Y. with permission of the author, reprinted from my pamphlet "How to Prevent Mixed Marriages.")

"CHRISTIANS who are not Roman Catholics have something that is quite as precious to them as the teaching of the Roman Church is to its members. Why should they not stand for the preciousness of their faith and resist the exactions of a Church which says, 'We make all the rules for any marriage in which one of our members is involved?' In a mixed marriage the Protestant or other non-Roman Christian is just as much involved as the Roman Catholic, and where his happiness and his freedom are concerned he must take a stand.

When intolerable conditions are introduced the young person should reject them even if it means delaying one's marriage until an equally attractive person of one's own faith can be found. With such a person the outlook for success will be distinctly more favorable. Most young people do not marry the first persons with whom they are in love. . . .

A Roman Catholic interprets marriage as one of the sacraments of his Church. He is taught that "a Catholic can be validly married only before a Catholic priest." The Protestant Christian thinks about marriage just as reverently, whether he calls it a sacrament or uses some other term. He thinks of it as instituted by God and perfected by God's blessing. He holds that it is God who joins the man and woman together by His grace and through their own sacred pledges to each other.

Marriage is an undertaking of two persons with God and with each other. In solemnizing it the minister acts as a representative of God and of the church. He is also the agent of the state for this particular purpose. The Protestant recognizes the authority both of the church and of the state, but repudiates the claim of one church that its priests have exclusive authority over his marriage when he marries a Roman Catholic. . . .

Recognizing that the Roman Catholic Church has the right under the freedom of religion to promulgate its teaching about marriage in any way it sees fit, we are compelled, in duty to those who look to us for counsel, to emphasize the fact that we of the other churches have freedoms and corrections that are inexpressibly precious to us. And we want to help our people in the safeguarding of these inheritances. . . .

ANTE-NUPTIAL AGREEMENT

(to be signed by the non-Catholic party in a mixed marriage)
I, the undersigned, not a member of the Catholic Church, wishing to contract marriage with . . . . ,
a member of the Catholic Church, propose to do so with the understanding that the marriage bond thus contracted is indissoluble, except by death. I promise on my word and honor that I will not in any way hinder or obstruct the said . . . .

in the exercise of .... religion and that all children of either sex born of our marriage shall be baptized and educated in the Catholic faith and according to the teaching of the Catholic Church, even though the said .... should be taken away by death. I further promise that I will marry .... only according to the marriage rite of the Catholic Church; that I will not either before or after the Catholic ceremony, present myself with .... for marriage before a civil magistrate or minister of the gospel.

Signature ....

Signed in the presence of Rev. ....

Place .... Date ....

Such demands mean that a Christian person who believes his own church to be a true church of Christ is asked, when he marries a Roman Catholic, to act as if his church were no church at all but a dangerous organization. He is required to proceed as if he had no faith in the adequacy of Jesus Christ as Saviour and Guide but rather must assume that only in the Roman Catholic Church could his children have assurance of Salvation.

Against such demands a man or woman of another church should set reasonable proposals of his own. When he is asked to submit to a course of instruction in Roman Catholic doctrine in order that he may understand the religious requirements of the person whom he is marrying, should he not ask the other to take a course under his church that the Roman Catholic person also may understand the life and ideals of the one whom he is marrying?

Our proposal is as reasonable as the other except to the

Roman Catholic who justifies a one-sided position by saying that, 'Truth has rights which error does not possess.' A Protestant might say the same thing if he were inclined to be equally arbitrary, but, on either part, it is merely begging the question to assume that one side has the truth and the other is in error. A home in which one has to be right while the other has to be wrong has a poor chance of a lasting, mutual esteem and of harmony.

When a Christian of another church is asked to sign an agreement that he will not interfere in the least with the free exercise of the Roman Catholic party's religion why should he not ask for a similar agreement in return? The present arrangement silences one party while encouraging in the other a proselytizing zeal. . . .

The Roman Catholic demands put the other member into a domestic straitjacket and in a measure alienates him from his children. It takes away the normal liberty of a loving parent of imparting to his child the truths that are deepest and dearest to him concerning God and His kingdom. This attitude is so utterly lacking in the conception of freedom of religious conviction that other Christians regard it as an attack upon their freedom of conscience. . . .

So long, however, as the Roman Church brands all other Christians as 'heretical' or 'schismatic' Roman Catholic individuals will be handicapped as marriage partners for members of other churches. . . . We cannot, however, without emphatic protest, allow the teaching that a mixed marriage solemnized by another minister is no real Christian marriage.

No more can we tolerate the idea that it is the duty of the Roman Catholic member to do everything possible through his home to proselyte while a Christian of another church must avoid even expressing his deepest religious convictions as if they were some kind of poison that would destroy his children. A Protestant or other non-Roman Christian who has found God in and through his church, and who in its fellowship has had communion with Christ, cannot for a moment tolerate the attitude of the Roman Catholic Church toward his faith.

We urge our young people to stand on their rights as self-respecting Christians who cannot in conscience submit to Roman Catholic domination. They should respect the freedom and the rights of all . . . but should stand firm against the requirements of a church which would handicap them in their family relationships."

CHAPTER NINE

Parochial Versus Public Schools

PART I

Official Catholic Instructions

"Catholics cannot approve of a system of education for youth apart from the Catholic Faith, and disjoined from the authority of the Church, and which regards primarily or prominently the knowledge of natural things, and the ends of social life.

"It is false that the best (educational) condition of civil society demands that Popular Schools open to the children of all classes, or that the generality of public institutions designed for letters and for the superior instruction and more extended cultivation of youth, should be free from all ecclesiastical authority, government and interference, and should be completely subjected to the Civil and Political Authority in conformity with the will of the rulers and the prevalent opinions of the age.

"It is necessary even in the present day that the Catholic religion shall be held as the only religion of the State, to the exclusion of all other forms of worship.

"Whence it has been unwisely provided by law, in some countries called Catholic, that persons coming to reside therein shall enjoy the free exercise of their religion.

"The civil liberty of every mode of worship, and full power given to all of openly and publicly manifesting their opinions and their ideas, conduce more easily to corrupt the morals and minds of the people, and to the propagation of the pest of indifferentism.

"The Roman Pontiff cannot and ought not to reconcile himself to, or agree with, Progress, Liberalism and Modern Civilization." —*From the Syllabus of Pope Pius IX, No.* 48, 47, 77, 78, 79, 80.

"Catholic Schools are to be most sedulously promoted, and it is to be left to the judgment and conscience of the ordinary (Bishop) to decide, according to the circumstances, when it is lawful to attend public schools" Pope Leo XIII to Cardinal Gibbons, May 31, 1893.

A part of the decree of the Third Plenary Council of Baltimore:

"We determine and decree:

"I. That by every church, where it does not already exist, a parochial school is to be erected within two years from the promulgation of this council (January 6th, Feast of Epiphany, 1886), and to be kept up in the future, unless the bishop sees fit to grant a further delay on account of more than ordinary grave difficulties to be overcome in its establishment.

"II. That a priest, who, within the aforesaid time, hinders, by serious negligence, the building and maintenance of a school, or does not regard the repeated admonitions of the bishop, deserves removal from that Church.

"III. That the mission or parish neglecting to aid the priest in the erection and support of a school, so that on account of this supine negligence the same cannot exist, is to be reprimanded by the bishop, and by every prudent and efficient means urged to supply the necessary helps.

"IV. That all Catholic parents are bound to send their children to parochial schools, unless they provide sufficiently and fully for their Christian education at home or at other Catholic schools. They may, however, be permitted for a good reason, approved by the bishop, and using meanwhile the necessary precautions and remedies, to send them to other schools. But it is left to the judgment of the ordinary to decide what is a Catholic school."

ROMAN CATHOLIC PARENTS MUST SEND THEIR CHILDREN TO PAROCHIAL SCHOOLS

To show the pressure put by Roman Catholic Officials upon parents to force them to send their children to parochial schools I quote from THE CATHOLIC TELEGRAPH—Cincinnati, Ohio—of August 25, 1904, the following letter, which represents the policy of the Roman Bishops in America from the Third Plenary Council of Baltimore—Jan. 6th, 1886—to the present time. The Pastoral letter reads as follows:

"To the Clergy and Laity of the Archdiocese of Cincinnati:

Dearly Beloved:

As the Catholic schools are about to open, We consider it

opportune to address you on the important obligation of parents to provide for the Catholic education of their children. There are, We regret to be obliged to say some fathers and mothers, who, either for the sake of fancied advantages, or through indifference, or on account of feeling against priest or teacher, send their children to non-Catholic schools.

It is undeniable, that as a rule, all Catholic teaching is excluded from non-Catholic schools and that in them there is usually present some kind of false religious influence. Now a system of education for the young, in which Catholic faith and the direction of the Church are excluded, can not be approved by any Catholic. The Church considers it vital to a child's faith, that the spirit of religion should animate every part of the scholar's task, and influence every hour of his time in school. The teachers should be good Catholics, well instructed in their faith, and be capable to thoroughly drill the children in religion. The Church recognizing this necessity has always opposed the separation of education and religion, and hence has condemned those who advocate it. . . . In the Encyclical of Leo XIII. 'Nobilissima' of the 8th of February, 1884, occur the following words: 'The Church has over and over again loudly condemned those schools which are called Mixed or Neutral, warning parents to be careful in a thing so momentous.'

These pronouncements of the Holy See are the law for all. The legislation of the III Plenary Council of Baltimore is based upon them. It is evident, then, that the doctrine of the church, which it would be erroneous, scandalous and even savoring of heresy to contradict, is that to attend a non-Catholic school constitutes usually a grave and permanent danger to faith, and that, therefore, it is a mortal sin for any parents to send their children to such a school, except where there is no other suitable school, and unless such precautions are taken as to make the danger remote.

In applying this teaching to practical life there are difficulties. We often meet with parents who object to sending their children to Catholic schools on account of certain features which they dislike or who prefer non-Catholic schools on account of certain advantages. They claim that, if they take due precaution to have their children properly instructed and brought up in piety, they can not justly be interfered with. But such a claim cannot be admitted. This is a religious question and is, therefore, within the sphere of the Church authority. In such questions it belongs to the Church not only to pronounce on the principle involved, but also on its application to particular cases and individual Catholics. It is the office of the Bishops, as the III Plenary Council of Baltimore teaches, to judge both of the alleged necessity, and of the sufficiency of the precaution. This is a matter, then, which lies within the jurisdiction of the spiritual power, and it is far from the true Catholic spirit to decide such a grave question for oneself.

Moreover, there is another aspect of the subject which shows still more clearly how necessary it is to abide by the judgment of the Church. It is almost impossible for a Catholic parent to send his child to a non-Catholic school anywhere in the country where there is a Catholic one without causing scandal. That is to say, such action suggests to other Catholic parents to do the same; it has the appearance of religious indifference; and it tends to break down the strictness and firmness of Catholic faith. It is, therefore, nearly always, a very grievous scandal especially when the parent in question is a person of some standing and influence. Now an action which involves scandal of this kind can only be justified by a very grave necessity. It is the duty of the parent, therefore, to take the judgment of the Church both upon the possible extent of the scandal and the reason for risking it. The foregoing principles justify us in laying down the following rules:

1. In places where there is a Catholic school parents are obliged under the pain of mortal sin to send their children to it. This rule holds good, not only in case of children who have not yet made their first Communion, but also in case of those who have received it. Parents should send their children to the Catholic school as long as its standards and grades are as good as those of the non-Catholic school. And even if there is no school attached to the congregation of which parents are members, they would still be obliged to send their children to a parochial school, college or academy, if they can do so without great hardships either to themselves or to their children.

2. It is the province of the Bishop to decide whether a parish should be exempted from having a parish school and whether, in case there be a Catholic in the place, parents may send their children to a non-Catholic school. Each case must be submitted to Us, except when there is question of children living three or more miles distant from a Catholic school. Such children can hardly be compelled to attend the Catholic school.

3. As the obligation of sending a child to a Catholic school binds under the pain of mortal sin, it follows that the neglect to comply with it, is a matter of accusation, when going to confession. We fail to see how fathers and mothers who omit to accuse themselves of this fault can believe that they are making an entire confession of their sins.

4. Confessors are hereby forbidden to give absolution to parents, who without permission of the Archbishop send their children to non-Catholic schools, unless such parents promise either to send them to the Catholic school, at the time to be

fixed by the Confessor, or, at least agree, within two weeks from the day of confession, to refer the case to the Archbishop, and abide by his decision. If they refuse to do either one or the other, the Confessor cannot give them absolution and should he attempt to do so, such absolution would be null and void. Cases of this kind are hereby numbered among the reserved cases from September 1, 1904.

5. The loss of Catholic training which the children suffer by being sent to non-Catholic schools must as far as possible be counteracted. Wherefore, we strictly enjoin that Diocesan Statute No. 64, be adhered to: 'We decree that those who are to be admitted to first holy Communion shall have spent at least two years in Catholic Schools. This rule is to be observed also by superiors of colleges and academies.' This Statute was enacted in Our Synod in 1898, and we regret that it has not always been observed. The necessity of complying with it is evident. It is difficult to properly prepare for first Communion even the children who have always attended Catholic schools; and it is simply impossible to do so when the children are allowed to go to non-Catholic schools up to a few months before they are to make their first holy Communion. Pastors, superiors of academies and colleges are admonished to observe this regulation. No exception is to be made to it without Our permission. In places where there is no Catholic school, Pastors will confer with Us as to the provision, which should be made for the instruction for first Communion.

6. Pastors seeking to prevent parents from taking their children too soon out of school have made regulations regarding the age of first Communion. As there has been some discrepancy in regard to this matter, some fixing one age, some a different one, and in consequence causing dissatisfaction among parents and children, We hereby direct that no child shall be ad-

mitted to first Communion, made publicly and solemnly, unless it has completed its thirteenth year on or before the day fixed for first Communion.

7. It is the Pastor's duty to decide whether the children of his parish have sufficient knowledge for making their first Communion. Hence, children attending a Catholic school other than the parish school, as well as those going to colleges and academies, must not be permitted to first Communion unless their Pastor has testified that they are sufficiently instructed for approaching the Holy Table. . . . Pastors will read this letter to their Congregations on the last Sunday in August.

May God bless all, and especially bless parents, their children and all engaged in the work of Catholic education.

Sincerely yours in Christ,
William Henry Elder,
Archbishop of Cincinnati.

Given at Cincinnati this 18th day of August."

PRIESTS HORRIFY ROMAN CATHOLIC PARENTS

Popes have given official instructions against public schools. Therefore Bishops have to bring pressure to bear upon Roman Catholic parents to force them to send their children to parochial schools. Moreover priests, who must obey without question, not only put pressure upon parents but HORRIFY them against sending their children to public schools.

The Rev. "Father" A. M. Skelly, O. P., with the permission of his superiors, printed a series of four discourses addressed to Catholic parents on the parochial school versus the public school, under the title, "Catholic Education or Where Do We Stand." Here are a few paragraphs:

"In looking over the programs of studies such as they are gone through in the schools of this country, we find that they divide the schools that follow them broadly into two classes. The ones are called secular or board schools—board schools, because school boards or committees are elected to take on the management of them; and secular schools, because the State authorities direct that only secular subjects shall be taught therein; the others are, in the main, our parochial or Catholic schools whose system is based on religion. To schools of the latter class you, my friends, are invited to send your children; whereas, the authorities of the Catholic Church forbid you as Catholics, and forbid you under severe penalties, except in case of grave necessity, to send your children to the former ones. This discrimination made by the bishops of the Catholic Church invites us to an examination into the reasons why they do so.

And I say that an investigation however superficial into the principles which guide the managing boards of the secular or public schools discloses the most cogent reasons why the superiors of the Catholic Church reject the teaching there given, and sanction and command the teaching given in the Catholic schools.

If we look to the beginnings of the educational system in this country we shall find that it had everywhere a religious basis. In Colonial days the life of the people was simple and primitive. The parental or common schools were supported by a tax which was allocated to the different schools of the district or municipality. And as the colonists of a district belonged ordinarily to the same religious denomination, there were little grounds for quarrel as to the teaching of religion.

SCHOOLS FOR THE POOR IRISH

However in the early years of the last century the more complex religious life of the great city of New York called for a modification of the school system as it had up to that time existed. A fifth part of the population of the metropolis was made up of poor Irish immigrants who came to the 'land of freedom' from persecution and misery at home. They were unable to support separate schools of their own, and they refused on religious grounds to send their children to schools where a religion alien to that which they themselves professed was inculcated. To meet this state of affairs the municipal council of the city countenanced the formation of a society to look after the education of the children of those submerged citizens. This was about the year 1805. With various changes and counterchanges as to the name of the new society, it finally took the title of *The Public School Society of New York.*

The society was supported in part by private subscription, which was collected in such a way as to give it the character of a closed corporation, but chiefly from funds donated to it from municipal and governmental sources, and it carried on its activities for many years.

At first religious instruction of a kind was permitted to be given to the children, but this permission was afterwards withdrawn, so that the Catholic Irish were left wholly neglected.

Seeing the unfairness of its workings the great Archbishop of New York, the Most Rev. John Hughes, carried on a suit before the municipal council, and afterwards before the legislative body of the state, sitting at Albany, petitioning the distribution of a *pro-rata* subsidy of the funds for the education of the Catholic children of his diocese. In this he was defeated, first, before the municipal council, and afterwards before the legislature, and this, I am ashamed to say, through the spirit of bigotry and intolerance that then obtained among the majority of the citizens and their Protestant pastors. From those days therefore a common school system of education without religion, copied after a deceitful model elaborated for his subjects by the crafty and autocratic-minded king of Prussia, was adopted and finally spread to the other States, till now we have all over the Union the notorious fetish to worship and admire, eclept, 'the Public School system of education of America.'

Religion may be inculcated or practised in the church, or in the home; but it has no place or tolerance in that imposing temple of secular and profane culture raised by a professedly Christian people—I mean the public school. *To such a den of worldiness and unreligion with its natural concomitants of the total suppression of the supernatural and the starvation of their spiritual faculties and aspirations, you, dearly beloved Catholic parents, are invited to entrust the jewels of your homes, the dear children given you by God to be formed to His knowledge and love.*

During the serious hours of the day, and throughout the whole formative period of their lives, you are so to devote your little ones. Within its halls their minds will be stocked with every conceivable branch of knowledge except that which will be really valuable to them for the life of the hereafter. The knowledge of God, of religion, and of Christian morality will be banned from their school lives, while the twin faculty of heart and will, will be allowed to run fallow, or to grow such vicious weeds of habit as they may pick up in their intercourse with one another and with the world. No account will be taken of the diseased condition of their souls consequent on their having been begotten of a fallen stock, and no helps of prayer or the Sacraments will be invoked or ministered to stay them amid the difficulties of life, or to repel the temptations coming from the world and the devil.

I ask you as responsible, Christian parents, as reasonable men and women, is this the kind of training you wish to procure for your children?

Stop!   Look!   Listen!

In the school your little ones will have to rub shoulders with the children coming from immoral and irreligious homes, children who know nothing of morality; from the homes of the divorcee, the infidel, and the pagan; children, it may be, of masterly dispositions, who will gain an ascendency over your little ones, but whose morals are often as corrupt as the dunghill.

When your children leave the Grammar School and enter the High School or University they will be confronted with the same agencies of worldliness and unreligion. Nay, here they will have greater difficulties to preserve their faith and morality; for they enter on the more perilous years of their mental development, *and the presentation of falsehood by their teachers* often becomes more aggressive, and is surrounded with a greater glamour of plausability. In those schools a sex knowledge is imparted which it ought not to be the function of the teachers to give, and this amid accompaniments which are often dangerous to morals. The blandishments of sex will have full sway by the freedom of intercourse allowed to boys and girls at the most unsteady period of life, blandishments which are enough to try the virtue of the strongest.

I will not here refer to evils that I have known, nor to the disasters that I could point to in the after years of men and women as a result of exposure during their formative years to influences such as I have described. I could point to the colossal disaster to the whole nation in the loss of religious belief in less than three generations of sixty per cent of the population, the descendants of those who seventy or eighty years ago were a deeply religious, if Protestant people. *All the impiety and irreligion that we witness in the United States today are in good part the evil fruits brought forth from the evil tree of a purely secular and Godless education....*

The histories tell us that one of the most dastardly things perpetrated by the miscreants of the French Revolution was to take the young Dauphin, the child of King Louis XVI and Marie Antoinette, and the heir to the proudest throne in Christendom, and to hand him over to a coarse and cruel cobbler; and in order to bring ridicule on the royal dignity, it was ordered that he be reared as a common rustic, to be kicked, and cuffed, and starved, and exposed to the jibes of the vilest elements of the population. The result was that he grew up a plebean and a clown, and afterwards disappeared among the populace. I ask you, is not the action of the Catholic parent who would send his child to the public school somewhat like that of the miscreants I have described? ...

Let me contrast briefly with this system of secular education, the Catholic system such as is carried on in your parochial schools, in the schools primary and advanced under the patronage of the church throughout America. ...

I would have you clearly understand that in the training thus of the faculties in religion the lessons given must not be looked on as mere school tasks. Religion is a life, a tradition, an atmosphere, which permeates the whole life of man, and is to be the chief incentive in all his other studies. In the education thus simultaneously of mind, and will, and heart, backed up by the Christian training of the inferior powers, which is according to the order of nature, (there is brought about a symmetry of development in those faculties which eventuates in perfect man). Moreover, their simultaneous culture helps and strengthens the one, the other. The aids of prayer and the Sacraments curb the impetuosity of the growing passions, and come to meet the deficiencies of nature and the disorder introduced into it by sin. As a result, we see that given equality of opportunity the pupils of the Catholic schools almost invariably outclass those raised in the public schools, turn out better balanced men and women, and more successful ones in meeting the difficulties that confront their after life in the world.

I speak not here at all of the intellectual and moral gifts of the teachers in the one or the other class of schools. I assume that in these qualifications they are without reproach. Where the superiority of the teachers in the Catholic schools comes in is that in this country they are almost invariably religious, men and women who have left the world to devote themselves solely to this great work of the education of the young; are themselves specialists in the science of religion, by the consecration of themselves to a life of perfection; and seek nothing in their service but the glory of God and the well-being, spiritual and temporal, of the children entrusted to them.

Let me conclude then by exhorting you as good Christian parents, first of all, to render thanks to Almighty God for the great benefit of having Catholic schools in your neighborhood to which you can without much inconvenience send your children; then, to send those children promptly to school on the opening day; to have them attend diligently throughout the scholastic year; and, lastly, to help financially your pastors, so that they may be enabled to keep your parochial schools in a good, efficient state, to pay a competent staff of teachers, and thus bring credit on yourselves and on them."

SHOULD OUR GOVERNMENT FINANCE ROMAN PAROCHIAL SCHOOLS?

The Protestant, or better the American, position against the pretentions of Romanism in favor of their parochial schools was very well defined by Bishop G. Bromley Oxnam of the Methodist Church of N. Y. in a pamphlet published Feb. 15, 1948 by the title "A Reply to Archbishop Cushing's Attack upon Protestants and other Americans united for the Separation of Church and State." I am quoting a few paragraphs:

"It is always hard for individuals reared in different religious cultures to understand each other. It would be ever so much better if we could sit round the table and, after prayer to our common Father and in the spirit of our common Saviour, discuss our common problems, and seek a common solution. I called upon Cardinal Spellman just a year ago, and proposed to him that such conferences be held. I told him that the tension between Protestant and Roman Catholic was to be deplored, but that we could not remove the tension by ignoring the causes that produce it. I had hoped that five or six leading members of the Roman Catholic hierarchy might sit in conference with a similar number from the Protestant communions and because we follow the same Christ, and are Americans, I had hoped that we might be able to reach some common understanding and thus be able to move together in an hour of crisis. Cardinal Spellman did not respond to the suggestion, either in the conference, or subsequently. I still believe this kind of conference continuing through the months would be valuable.

It is, as I say, hard to understand each other when reared in different cultures. . . . .

The question of public funds for private or sectarian education is one of great importance. This nation, by democratic decision, created a public educational system, believing that a democratic government must be based upon an intelligent and patriotic people. This educational opportunity is made available to all. It is indeed of the people, by the people, and for the people. I regard the public educational system as one of the great achievements of American history. It is a bulwark of democracy. I know of no more patriotic, devoted, and inspiring group than the teachers of the American public schools. These teachers have come from our homes, our churches, our colleges. It is my privilege each year to address many thousands of them. I think I know them. When I hear individuals criticize our public schools and use such terms as 'godless' and 'immoral,' I know that they are either unacquainted with the public school system or have ulterior ends in mind. From long acquaintance with the public school, I am convinced that the product of our public schools, when compared with the product of private and sectarian schools, will hold its own in terms of idealism, morality, love of country, democratic spirit, and intellectual attainment. This school system must be protected and improved. I served as a member of the President's Commission on Higher Education, and had some opportunity to become acquainted with those aspects of our work that need improvement. The fact that we face our school system realistically and plan for its continuous improvement is but another evidence of its success. More than thirty million Americans are in our public schools. The President's Commission considered the demands of the Roman Catholic Church for support of sectarian education from public funds, and voted overwhelmingly to support the principle that public funds shall be used solely for public education.

I believe in the American public school system where my Protestant sons and daughter sat in classrooms with their Roman Catholic friends, Jew by Gentile, black by white, foreign-born by native-born, and learned how to live together. There they came to know each other as human beings, not as Protestants, Roman Catholics, Jews, and Gentiles, black and white, but as children of one Father. That, to me, is better than the Roman way which takes a part of the children away from the public school system and puts them in a private or sectarian system. This is simply an expression of my personal preference. I grant fully the right of the Roman Catholic to maintain his schools, if he desires; but I insist that he must pay for them. Why? If we grant to the Roman Catholic the right to maintain a parochial system and then, in addition, call upon the public to support the system, we are saying immediately to the Methodist Church, the Baptist Church, and to all other Communions, you, too, may set up your own system of sectarian education. What is the result of this? It is to drain off vast sums from the support of public education, thereby to weaken the public system, and I think eventually to destroy it. The Roman Catholic Church does not believe in our public system.

The President's Report states:

'Federal funds for the general support of current educational activities and for general capital outlay purpose should be appropriated for use only in institutions under public control.

'Sound public policy demands, furthermore, that State and local public educational bodies be able to exercise at all times the right to review and control educational policies in any institution or agency for which public monies are appropriated and expended. Public responsibility for support of education implies public responsibility for the policies which are supported.'

The position of the Roman Catholic Church in terms of principle is stated with frankness in a pamphlet entitled 'Freedom of Worship, the Catholic Position,' written by Francis J. Connell, C. SS. R., S. T. D. This is published by the Paulist Press, and carries the imprimatur of Francis J. Spellman, Archbishop of New York, recently made a Cardinal. 'The Catholic Church is the only organization authorized by God to teach religious truth and to conduct public religious worship. Consequently, they (Catholics) hold that any creed which differs from that of the Catholic Church is erroneous, and that any religious organization which is separated from the Catholic Church lacks the approval and the authorization of God. The very existence of any other church is opposed to the command of Christ that all men should join His one church. From this it follows that, as far as God's Law is concerned, no one has a real right to accept any religion save the Catholic religion, or to be a member of any church save the Catholic Church, or to practice any form of divine worship save that commanded or sanctioned by the Catholic Church . . . Logically, then, Catholics hold that no one has a genuine right, as far as God's law is concerned, to profess any religion except the Catholic religion. Certainly, no creature has a genuine right to disobey the commands of God. . . . It was in accord with this principle that Pope Pius IX, in his Syllabus of 1864, condemned the proposition: 'Every man is free to embrace and to profess that religion which, guided by the light of reason, he judges true.' . . . The mere fact that a person sincerely believes a religion to be true gives him no genuine *right* to accept that religion in opposition to God's command that all must embrace the one true religion. Neither does it necessarily oblige others to allow him the unrestricted practice of his religious beliefs. . . . The second Catholic principle, pertinent to freedom of worship, can be called, by contrast to the first, the principle of *personal tolerance.* . . . Catholics may not persecute non-Catholics because of their sincere religious convictions. However, as was pointed out above, this does not necessarily imply that unrestricted freedom must be granted by Catholics to the religious activities of non-Catholics. . . . If the country is distinctively Catholic—that is, if the population is almost entirely Catholic, and the national life and institutions are permeated with the spirit of Catholicity —the civil rulers can consider themselves justified in restricting or preventing denominational activities hostile to the Catholic religion. . . . They are justified in repressing written or spoken attacks on Catholicism, the use of the press or the mails to weaken the allegiance of the Catholics toward their church, and similar anti-Catholic efforts. . . . Nevertheless, even in a predominantly Catholic country, circumstances may render it more advisable for the government to grant non-Catholics the same measure of freedom of worship as is enjoyed by Catholics.'

That, no doubt, is the Roman Catholic position. It is not the Protestant position. . . .

May I conclude with a plea for conference and the end of controversy, for cooperation rather that conflict, in a word, for the acceptance of Christ not alone in creedal statement but in daily conduct."

PART II

Catholic-Protestant School Battle in the Press

QUICK magazine, N. Y., N. Y., published the pictures of Cardinal Spellman and Bishop Oxnam on the cover of July 11, 1949 issue and outlined the school controversy as follows:

BATTLE OF THE WEEK SHOULD U.S. FUNDS AID CHURCH SCHOOLS?

YES—Francis Cardinal Spellman, Archbishop of N. Y. *(front cover)*: "We must not stand idly by and watch our Government spend $300,000,000 according to legislation that would be unjust and discriminatory. . . . We must oppose any bill that fails to guarantee at least non-religious textbooks, bus rides and health services for all children."

Sen. George D. Aiken, R., Vt.: "I favor a substantial measure of Federal aid for private schools, for such purposes as transportation of pupils, health programs and purchase of non-religious supplies."

The Rev. Laurence J. McGinley, S. J., president, Fordham University: "If parents have the right to send their children to any adequate school . . . then obviously all these schools must be allowed to exist without unfair discrimination or undue favoritism."

Sen. Brien McMahon, D., Conn.: "A child shall not be counted in for ascertaining the amount [of Federal funds for education] . . . then, if he happens to attend a non-public school, be counted out."

NO—Methodist Bishop G. Bromley Oxnam *(front cover):*

"To drain off vast public sums from the support of public education in order to support parochial education will destroy the public system."

Federal Council of the Churches of Christ in America: "We affirm our continued adherence to the American principle of the separation of church and state, and to the principle that public funds should not be used for sectarian purposes."

Mrs. Eleanor Roosevelt: "Those of us who believe in the right of any human being to belong to whatever church he sees fit . . . cannot be accused of prejudice when we do not want to see public education connected with religious control of the schools."

Central Conference of American Rabbis: "Schools that are maintained solely to preserve and advance any particular religious faith, be it Jewish or Christian, should be maintained out of private, not public, resources."

THE CHURCHMAN magazine, N. Y., N. Y. editorialized the school battle in the July issue, 1949 under the title:

THE ROMANS ARE WORRIED

"Cardinal Spellman, and the Roman hierarchy for which he speaks, is worried. The Roman church believes, correctly, that the Barden Bill, H. R. 4643, which provides federal aid only to tax-supported public schools, will probably pass, in spite of strong Roman pressures brought against it. It will be recalled that one of the primary objectives announced in the original Manifesto of Protestants and Other Americans United for Separation of Church and State was to mobilize public opinion against the use of public funds for sectarian and private schools.

On Sunday, June 19, Cardinal Spellman spoke to 15,000 Catholics at Fordham University. His address was devoted to a denunciation of Representative Graham A. Barden and the federal aid bill for public schools he is sponsoring. Calling the congressman a 'new apostle of bigotry,' and his supporters in Congress 'disciples of discrimination,' the cardinal said that they were venting 'venom upon children' in 'a sin as shocking as it is incomprehensible.' To establish a pious smoke-screen, he asked his hearers to pray for 'one who, because of his sponsorship of un-American, anti-Catholic legislation, deserves in my opinion to be linked in American history with the names of others guilty of disservice to our country and the multiple peoples and principles that make our nation consecrate.' He charged that the congressman was 'violating and inciting others to violate the very rights and freedom upon which our democratic government was found.' "

Bishop G. Bromley Oxnam, vice-president of Protestants and Other Americans United, was quick to label Spellman's description of the Barden bill correctly. He said that to designate it as a "crusade of religious prejudice is to lie." Dr. Oxnam's statement was as follows:

'Congressman Graham Barden of North Carolina deserves the commendation of the country rather than the condemnation of a cardinal. As a loyal and wise legislator Representative Barden insists upon the American principle that public funds shall be used solely for public education.'

Cardinal Spellman has used the term 'bigot' freely of late. Now we know what he means by it. Anyone who disagrees with the cardinal or who objects to the hierarchy putting its hands in the public treasury is a bigot.

Cardinal Spellman belittles himself when he refers to Representative Barden as "un-American and anti-Catholic," or as venting "his venom upon children," or "as guilty of disservice to our country." This is bearing false witness and to describe the bill as "conducting a craven crusade of religious prejudice" is to lie.

To drain off vast public sums from the support of public education to support parochial education will destroy the public system. Barden wants to preserve public education and to send Federal aid to underprivileged areas for public schools. It is not "putting class against class" or a "vote against constitutional right." It is the preservation of American public education and its protection from a prelate with a prehensile hand.

Incidentally, in *The New York Times*, Cardinal Spellman's statement was given a front-page position, under a two-column headline. On the day Dr. Oxnam's reply was printed it rated the twenty-fifth page. The three Roman Catholics who daily make up the *Times* followed a characteristic practice. In the *Herald Tribune* a few sentences from the statement made page 21.

Commenting on Spellman's statements, Dr. Glenn L. Archer, executive secretary of POAU, said: "Representative Barden's bill . . . is the only kind of a bill which fully accords with the concept of religious freedom bequeathed to this nation by Thomas Jefferson, who said, 'To compel a man to furnish contributions of money for propagation of opinions which he disbelieves is sinful and tyrannical.' The archbishops' latest blast is the most recent evidence of a well-organized campaign to destroy the American system of free public education. There is nothing in the Barden Bill which deprives any church from sponsoring its own schools for reasons peculiar to the need of that church. Since the majority of the Roman Catholic children now attend public school, the Barden Bill is not anti-Catholic."

If any of our readers are inclined to swallow the cardinal's words, we trust that they will look up statements of Roman leaders and the Roman press on our public schools. Many such sources are quoted in Paul Blanshard's recent volume, *American Freedom and Catholic Power*. A typical statement is that from the pamphlet by Paul L. Blakely, S. J., "May an American Oppose the Public School," which bears the imprimatur of the late Cardinal Hayes.

For example: "Our first duty to the public school is not to pay taxes for its maintenance. . . . The first duty of every Catholic father to the public school is to keep his children out of it. . . . For the man who sends his children to the public school when he could obtain for them the blessings of a Catholic education is not a practicing Catholic, even though he goes to mass every morning. . . . 'Every Catholic child in a Catholic school' is the command of the church."

The position against the Roman demands for aid to parochial schools is in accord with federal and state constitutions, and is upheld by the Supreme Court of the United States. If you oppose such aid, and to having *your* money used for Roman Schools, write to your congressmen and to Mr. Barden. And don't be misled by the Roman charge that in so doing, you are a "bigot" or "anti-Catholic." *It's time for Protestants and other non-Roman Americans to wake up to the fact that such charges are the most useful defence line employed by the Roman hierarchy*. It has not yet become "anti-Catholic" to be pro-American.—The Churchman

U.S. ON ALERT AGAINST PAROCHIAL SCHOOLS

The case of North College Hill, Cincinnati, Ohio on April 15, 1947.

Twenty-nine of thirty-three teachers gave their resignations because the one-man Roman Catholic majority on the local

board of education had unloaded the North College Hill parochial school, including its teaching staff of eight nuns, on the
public treasury for its entire support. Each month a substantial
check is made out to Archbishop McNicholas for the rental of
the school at the rate of $6,000 a year, and separate payments
are made to the nuns. But the school board majority was not
satisfied to stop there. It adopted a course of action which has
completely disrupted the public school system of the community.
Today North College Hill has no school superintendent, only
a handful of teachers, and with the exception of the parochial
school and a school for Negro children in an affiliated subdistrict,
its school system is disrupted and wrecked.

The superintendent of schools, Dr. William A. Cook was
charged with "insubordination" and ousted.

He refused repeatedly to turn over to the board his confi-
dential files of teacher applications and the correspondence relating to them.

The conflict reached its climax over the issue of who should
nominate new teachers for the public schools. If the Catholic
board members could get control of this function, which is
placed by law in the hands of the superintendent, they could
flood the schools with Catholic teachers and so put the entire
system into the hands of the church.

The board's resignation placed the administration of the
schools in the hands of Probate Judge Chase M. Davies of Cincinnati.

After holding public hearings, Judge Davies reappointed
Dr. William A. Cook as superintendent of schools in North
College Hill for a three-year term. Dr. Cook accepted and 24 of
the 29 teachers who had resigned signed new contracts. The

others had accepted work elsewhere. An election was to be held that fall to determine the personnel of the new school board, which would take office January 1, 1948. Simultaneously the issue of control of the Cincinnati board of education would be determined in a city-wide election, with the seats of two Protestant members at stake.

The Roman Catholic clerical program to invade the public school system in North College Hill must be understood as a local spearhead of a nationwide movement to gain control of and to rule for their own advantage the free public schools of America.

—For more information about this case write to the Christian Century Press, 407 So. Dearborn St., Chicago 5, Ill.

ROMAN CATHOLICS LOSE NEW
MEXICO SCHOOL CASE

The Case of Dixon, New Mexico., March 1949

The decision in the legal action brought against some 200 defendants, including Catholic nuns, brothers, priests, bishops, and state officers, by Protestants, Roman Catholics and others of Dixon, New Mexico, was a victory, in the first round, for the plaintiffs.

The presumption is that the case will be taken to the Supreme Court of the state by the Roman Catholic bishops and their co-defendants. This, despite the cost which will continue to be high to the plucky folks of Dixon, will be welcomed by them and many in different parts of the country who have helped them so far. The final decision must be clear-cut, even if it has to be taken to the United States Supreme Court.

The sisters and brothers of their respective orders did all

they could to cover up the facts that had been testified to by the witnesses for the plaintiffs. Some of the testimony of the Roman Catholic orders, as represented by their teachers in the 29 schools where they taught, in light of the facts was humorous if it did not excite pity in some who heard it. Their faith is so strong, the influence of their bishops over them so great, and the moral theology of the church so deficient that it was not as difficult for some of them to shade the truth as it would be for one reared under the strict teaching of Protestant denominations. One of the nuns did testify that she taught the pupils that it was a sin to engage in any exercise that was not approved by the Catholic Church.

District Judge E. Turner Hensley held in his decision that Catholicism is taught in some of the state's public schools contrary to both the state and Federal Constitutions. He added: "There is no separation of Church and State in the places named." The Judge's apt remark was obviously prompted by the testimony of three nuns on the public pay roll who readily admitted on the witness stand that they taught catechism.

COURT BANS PAY FOR SCHOOL BUS

The Case of Mankato, Minnesota.

Refund order by Judge Gislason, Mankato, Minn., May 23, 1949—A school district cannot pay for the transportation of pupils to parochial schools, even though the district's own school is closed, District Judge A. B. Gislason of New Ulm held in an order issued here.

Gislason issued an injunction halting school district 140 of Blue Earth country from paying for the transportation of pupils from LeRay township to parochial schools in Mankato and Madison Lake.

The order stated that 15 pupils have been transported from LeRay township, where the school is closed, to All Saints school in Madison Lake and 14 parochial schools in Mankato daily.

Only nine pupils from the township are attending public grade schools and one public high school in Mankato, according to the order.

NUNS TEACHING IN NEW HAVEN SCHOOLS

Cases in Connecticut and Michigan.

New Haven, Connecticut, April 1949—In two of this city's public schools *twenty-two Roman Catholic sisters* are members of the teaching staffs. Although they wear religious garb, they teach regular grade school subjects, and *their salaries are paid out of public school funds.*

In the Hamilton Street school (with 888 pupils and thirty teachers) *fifteen of the staff, including the principal, are Sisters of Mercy.*

In the Highland Heights school (with 305 pupils and ten teachers) seven of the staff, including the principal, are members of the same order.

A recent evaluation survey of the public school system recommends that this arrangement be allowed to continue during the tenure of the present teaching sisters, and that they then be replaced by regular teachers. *Inasmuch as the sisters have life tenure, the situation is not likely to change soon.*

Lansing, Mich., June 1949 [RNS]—Veto of the Phillips Bill, which would broaden a 1945 law permitting transportation of private or parochial school pupils in public school buses, was urged here upon Governor G. Mennen Williams by a delegation of Protestant and Jewish groups. The bill has been approved by the state legislature.

John H. McPherson, Detroit attorney, representing the Grosse Pointe Unitarian church and the Michigan Committee to Maintain the Separation of Church and State, said the "bill is ill-considered" and "violates a longstanding tradition of the state and the national policy of separation of Church and State on school affairs." McPherson told the governor that "a majority would back your veto."

Dr. J. Burt Bouwman, executive secretary of the state church council, termed the bill "a beginning which might lead to further difficulties," and urged veto as the "only clear way to avoid those difficulties."

Sam Brown, Detroit regional director for the American Jewish Congress, said, "It looks harmless but may not be. The better way is to veto it and have a complete analysis."

NUNS DON CIVILIAN DRESS TO TEACH IN DAKOTA SCHOOL

The Case of North Dakota.

Nuns in modern dress are ringing school bells in a dozen North Dakota communities this week.

So they can continue teaching in public schools this year, about 60 of them are discarding the voluminous black habits they have worn since they first took the veil.

By a margin of 11,500 votes North Dakotans last summer approved an initiated act to prohibit public school teachers from wearing garb denoting membership in any religious order. Sponsored by a group of Protestant ministers, the measure was aimed chiefly at the 74 nuns teaching in North Dakota's public schools.

In a surprise announcement, the Catholic church then said the nuns could continue to teach in civilian clothing if they wanted to and if the local school boards still wanted them.

About 60 of the 74 are going to do so, a survey by The Associated Press revealed.

Though the state department of public instruction said it would have no figures on the changeover until late next year, this appeared to be the situation:

In 12 of the 19 public schools where the sisters taught last year, they will continue to teach in civilian dress.

Five of the 19 schools are converting to parochial Catholic schools thus losing public tax support. In two communities, this means converting just one room in an otherwise all-parochial school.

At two schools, Gladstone and Olga, the sisters are quitting as teachers.

A Catholic leader today said the garb issue "had nothing to do with their withdrawal from these two schools. Two years ago the sisters proposed to leave Gladstone but remained only because other teachers could not be found to take their place. They had signified their intention of withdrawing from both Olga and Gladstone before the garb issue was placed before the people."

Several Catholic leaders have taken the position that permitting nuns to wear secular dress is making passage of the anti-garb bill a hollow victory for its sponsors.

The sponsors have maintained official silence since the church announced this move.

A Protestant clergyman who helped sponsor the law said that its purpose had been achieved.

"We accomplished what we set out to do—remove the cultural and denominational atmosphere of any specific religion from the public school classroom," he said.

Part III

Should Roman Catholics Teach in Our Public Schools?

The Roman Church—popes, bishops, priests, and laymen—do not hesitate in opposing and denouncing our public schools. Then why should the followers of Romanism be allowed to teach in public schools?

Would you employ in your business a man who would tell your customers that your merchandise is rotten and that they should buy from his relatives' store? And would you want to finance that rival store?

No business man in his right mind would do this. Yet our government is not only employing teachers who are privately and publicly against our educational system, but is considering the financing of private Roman Catholic schools.

If the public schools of this country are not good enough for the children of Roman Catholic parents, then the true American parents should consider their children too good to be taught by Roman Catholic teachers. I am referring, of course, to Roman Catholics who take orders from the Vatican.

Let us see if we should trust our children to the followers of Romanism. Every loyal Roman Catholic accepts and follows the moral theology of St. Alfonsus de Liguori, since it has been officially approved and recommended by the Roman Church.

St. Alphonsus Mary de Liguori was canonized—that is enrolled among the Saints in heaven by the pronunciation of Pope Gregory XVI—year 1839 and declared a Doctor of the Universal Roman Church by Pius IX.

The congregation of Sacred Rites stated that they had examined his manuscripts and printed works, and that there was "nothing censurable in any thing St. Alphonsus de Liguori had written."

"Such are the doctrines of that Saint; I shall say, with Cardinal Gousset, of that wise and holy Doctor, whose opinions, taught by him in his 'Moral Theology,' it is lawful to embrace and profess (Decision of the Sacred Penitentiary of July 5, 1835); whose writings contain nothing worthy of censure (Decree of Pope Pius VII, 1803), and the faithful may saturate themselves (empaparse) in them *percurri a fidelibus*, without the least peril, *inoffenso prorsus pede* (Bull of canonization). The doctrines of this Saint are now the doctrines, not only of Italy, but of Europe and of the Catholic world. And if any one should undertake to obscure his splendour he would be committing a folly as great as that of trying to obscure the light of the sun."—page XIV, XV Spanish edition of Moral Theology of Liguori.

In consequence of that, there is in the breviary, and also in the missal, which every Roman Catholic is bound to use—the following prayer for the 2d day of August:—

"Oh God, who, by the blessed Alphonsus, thy Confessor and Pontiff, inflamed with the love of souls, hast enriched thy church with a new offspring, we implore that, taught by his instructions, and strengthened by his example, we may be able to come to thee through the Lord."

Every Roman Catholic, then, prays that he may be strengthened by the example and taught by the instructions of the blessed Saint Liguori. He is a general authority—"A catholic authority." The Saint and Doctor teaches that:

A CATHOLIC CAN LIE

"Notwithstanding, indeed, although it is not lawful to lie, or to feign what is not, however it is lawful to dissemble what is, or to cover the truth with words, or other ambiguous and doubtful signs, for a just cause, and when there is not a necessity of confessing. Est Comm. S. Thom. Kon. dis. 15. dub. 2. n. 9. Laym. 1. 2. t. i. c. 11." [Vol. 2. B. 3. ch. 3. p. 116.]

"These things being settled, it is a certain and a common opinion among all divines, that for a just cause it is lawful to use equivocation in the modes propounded, and to confirm it (equivocation) with an oath. Less. 1. 2. c. 41. n. 47. Card. diss. 19. n. 35. Salm. tr. 17. de Juram. cap. 2. n. 115. ex. S. Hieron. c. 22. q. 2." [Vol. 2. B. 4. treat. 2. p. 316.]

"But probably enough Lugo de Just. d. 40. n. 15. Tamb. lib. 3. c. 4. § 3. n. 5. cum Sanch. Viva q. 7. art. 4. n. 2. Sporer de Praec. c. 1. num. 13. item Elbel dict. num. 144. Card. in Propt. Innoc. XI. diss. 19. num. 78. cum Nav. Less. Sa, et Fill. with many others, say, that the accused, if threatened with death, or imprisonment, or perpetual exile, the loss of all property, the galleys, and such like, can deny the crime, even with an oath (at least without great sin), by understanding that he did not commit it, *so that he is bound to confess it,* only let there be a hope of avoiding the punishment." [Vol. 2. p. 34.]

"He who has accepted a loan, but has afterward returned it, can deny that he received the loan, understanding *so as that he ought to pay it.* Salm. n. 140. et Sporer de 2. Praec. c. 1. n. 122. cum Suar. Nav. Az. Laym. Sanch. Cov. and others." [Ibid. 322.]

"He who comes from a place falsely supposed infections, can deny that he came from that place, to wit, *as from a pestilent place,* because this is the mind of the *cordon sanitaire.* Salm. n. 141. Les. cap. 42. n. 47. Sanch. Dec. lib. 3. cap. 6. n. 35. et Sporer, loc. sit. n. 140. cum Tol. Nav. Suar. Henr. Rod. etc."

"If any one invited to dine, is asked if the food which is in fact unpalatable be good, he can answer, *It is good,* to wit, *for mortification.*"

"It is asked, 5,—Whether a servant, by the order of his master can deny that he [the master] is at home. Card. diss. 19. n. 75. admits that he can feign his master's foot on the step, and answer, *He is not here,* because it is not mental restriction; but to this I do not assent, if the other can by no means understand that. Rather I would concede that he can say, *He is not here,* that is to say, *not in this door or window,* or, (as Tourn. Mor. tom. i. page 689,) *He is not here so as that he may be seen.* Also Carden says that he can answer that *he has departed from the house,* by understanding a departure which took place in some time past; for we are not bound, he says, with Lessius, as above, to answer to the mind of him that interrogates, if there is a just cause." Ibid. 525.

"It is certain that if you transgress only some small part of what you have sworn, it is not a grievous sin: for example, if you have sworn that you would not drink wine, you did not sin mortally in drinking a very little, (Sanch. t. 1. lib. 4. c. 32, n. 21,) because then the smallness of the matter excuses; and thus they are excused who swear to observe the statutes of some chapter, college, university, etc., if afterwards they violate the statutes in some small way. And we say the same concerning sworn public registrars and other ministers of justice; as also concerning him who, from the sum which he swore that he would give to another should subtract only a little. Navar. Suar. Sanch. Vide Laym. Bon. p. 13.

"Probably you are obliged by a promissory oath, although it may be extorted from you by injury and fear, as if, forgetting to use equivocation, you promised to robbers to give booty, or usury to usurers."

"Nevertheless, make an exception if you have sworn to Titias to marry her; for in that case you can forsake her, and enter a religious order: because the oath regards the nature of the act to which it pertains; but in the promise of matrimony there is this tacit condition, *unless I enter a religious order.*" See Laym. c. 6. Bon. d. 4. q. 1. p. 3. [Ibid. p. 337.]

A CATHOLIC CAN STEAL

"If any one on an occasion should steal only a moderate sum either from one or more, not intending to acquire any notable sum, neither to injure his neighbor to a great extent, by several thefts, he does not sin grievously, nor do these, taken together, constitute a mortal sin; however, after it may have amounted to a notable sum by detaining it, he can commit mortal sin, but even this mortal sin may be avoided, if either then he be unable to restore, or have the intention of making restitution immediately of those things which he then received."

"Query II. If small thefts which together amount to a large sum, be made from various known masters, whether a thief be bound under great blame to make restitution to them, or whether he may satisfy by distributing them to paupers? On the one hand it appears that a restitution should be made to the original possessors, unless the danger of losing fame, or very grievous loss, or inconvenience excuse."

"Whence it appears that a thief may have rendered sufficient satisfaction to his own weighty obligation from the presumed consent of the republic, if he make restitution to paupers, or pious places which are the more needy parts of the republic." Vol. 3, page 258.

Officially interpreting the above doctrine, Roman Catholic authorities in America informed Roman Catholics that it is not a sin to steal less than $40.00, at one time. Thus, according to this teaching, $39.00 may be stolen from a thousand or any number of people without committing a grave offence—mortal sin—In the Jan. 1945, issue of The American Ecclesiastical Review, official magazine of instruction for priests published at Catholic University in Washington, D.C., on page 68 we read:

"Question: What would be regarded nowadays as the absolute sum for grave theft in the United States?" "Answer: By the absolute sum for grave theft is meant that amount of money, the stealing of which constitutes a mortal sin, irrespective of the financial status of the individual or corporation from whom it is taken, however wealthy they may be. Naturally this sum varies with the fluctuation of the value, or the purchasing power, of money. In a large country like ours it is quite possible that this sum might be different in different sections. To lay down a general norm, in view of actual conditions and the value of money, it would seem that the absolute sum for grave theft would be about $40.00—Francis J. Connell, C.S.S.R.

Now back again to St. Alfonsus:

"It is lawful for a son to rejoice at the murder of his parent committed by himself in a state of drunkenness, on account of the great riches acquired by inheritance." —St. Alfonsus, 1, 5, 21.

"To curse the living is a mortal sin, when it is formal, that is, when he who curses intends and wishes a grievous evil to befall the one he curses; but it is no mortal sin to curse the living when the curse pronounced is merely material. It is not a mortal sin to curse the dead."   —St. Alfonsus, 1, 3, n-130.

"A servant is allowed to help his master to climb a window to commit fornication."—1, 22, 66.   "Open the door and bring gifts to his paramour."   —St. Alfonsus, n,45.

"It is not a mortal sin to get drunk, unless one loses completely the use of his mental faculties for over one hour." —1, 5, 75.

"It is lawful to violate penal laws (hunting, fishing, traffic laws, etc.)."

"It is lawful to wish evil under the condition if it were licit. So a priest may wish to marry a beautiful girl under the condition if he were not a priest."—St. Alfonsus Hom. Apost. Tract, 3n. 50

"It is lawful for confessors cautiously to speak to women when it is necessary, and to kiss and embrace them according to the custom of the country, if by refraining from it they would be considered uncivil."—St. Alfonsus, 3, n. 381.

"Gambling is allowed."—St. Alfonsus, 3, n. 879.

"It is asked whether prostitutes are to be permitted . . . they are to be permitted because, as a distinguished priest says, 'Remove prostitutes from the world, and all things will be disordered with lust.' Hence in large cities, prostitutes may be permitted."—St. Alfonsus, 3, 434.

It is enough! Would you trust your children to the followers of the above doctrines? If you would, then you are willing to have their morals undermined. Roman Catholics do not get their morals from the Bible, but rather accommodate them to this wicked world in which we live.

CHAPTER TEN

List of Roman Catholic Terms

Abbess: the superioress of nuns who holds an office correspond-ing to that of an abbot in communities of men. She bears a ring, pectoral cross, and pastoral staff which symbolize her dignity. She has full domestic authority but unlike the abbots has no spiritual powers.

Abbot: the superior, or head, of Benedictines, Cistercians, or other monks. He is elected for life, is blessed by the bishop after election, wears a ring and pectoral cross, may pontificate at mass, using the crosier and throne, he may confer minor orders, and has complete authority over his monks who live as a family in a settled location.

Ad limina visits: visits of the bishops to the tombs of the Apos-tles Peter and Paul in Rome every three to ten years. On the occasion of these visits the bishops give a report on their dioceses to the Pope.

Advent: a period of four weeks of preparation and penance be-fore Christmas. It recalls the thousands of years of waiting before the arrival of the promised Redeemer, commemorated by Christ-mas.

Anglican Orders: The invalid orders (ordination of priests and bishops) conferred by bishops of the Anglican Church. They were pronounced invalid by Pope Leo XIII in 1896.

Annunciation: the message of the angel informing the Blessed Virgin that she was chosen to be the Mother of God. The Incarnation took place on this same occasion. The event is commemorated on March 25.

Apostolic Delegate: One who represents the Roman Pontiff in a country whose government has no diplomatic relations with the Holy See.

Archbishop: The bishop of an archdiocese, who has certain authority, as determined by canon law, over the bishops of a section of the country usually called a province.

Assumption: The teaching of the Church that Mary's body, without undergoing the corruption of the grave, was reunited to her glorious soul, and that in this state Mary was taken into heaven.

Banns of marriage: Announcement of an intended marriage on three different Sundays or holydays in the church or churches of the parties, in order that those who know of any existing impediment to the marriage, may bring it to the attention of the pastor making the announcement.

Beatification: Declaration by the Pope, as Head of the Church, that a member of the Church is to be regarded as dwelling in heaven and as deserving of public veneration.

Biretta: A stiff square cap with three ridges and a tuft on the top worn by the clergy.

Breviary: The book containing the prayers which priests and those in sacred orders or nuns must say daily.

Bull: A name given to the most solemn and important letters of the Pope. So named from the "bulla" or seal attached to the letter.

Canon Law: A collection of the laws of the Church. The New Code of Canon Law is divided into five sections and contains in all 2414 canons of laws.

Canonization: A Declaration of the Holy See decreeing that a person who has already been beatified be regarded as a Saint and venerated everywhere. Two major miracles through the intercession of the person occurring after the beatification are necessary for canonization.

Cassock: A close fitting garment, worn by clerics, reaching to the heels and fastened down the front with buttons. The word comes from the Italian "casacca" meaning "great coat".

Catafalque: A framework of wood outside of the Communion railing covered with a black pall, surrounded by six candles, and symbolizing the corpse at a requiem mass.

Celebret: ("Let him celebrate")—A document, issued by a bishop or religious superior, showing that the one who carries it is a priest and deserving of being permitted to say Mass.

Chancery office: The bishop's office which carries on the administration of the diocese and handles diocesan business.

Church (*of women*): The saying of a prayer of thanksgiving to God by a priest over a woman who has given birth to a child, and the imparting of a blessing to her.

Conclave: The place where the Cardinals assemble to elect a new Pope, or the assembly of the Cardinals itself which elects the Pope.

Concordat: A treaty or agreement between the Holy See and a civil power in regard to religious matters.

Consistory: An assembly of Cardinals and sometimes of others summoned by the Pope to discuss Church affairs of great importance.

Degradation: A rite whereby a cleric in punishment is deposed from his office, is deprived of his clerical dress, and is reduced to the lay state. A degraded priest retains his priestly character and remains bound by the obligations of the priesthood.

Diocese: A definite territory with its population governed by a Bishop.

Divine Office, The: The text of the Breviary consisting of psalms, prayers, hymns and readings. The recitation of this text by all clerics in major orders constitutes the public and official prayer of the Church.

Doctor of the Church: Title conferred by the Pope or a General Council on a saint whose writings show profound learning and freedom from error.

Dogma: A revealed truth contained in Scripture or Tradition, and infallibly accepted or defined by the Church.

Easter Duty: The obligation of Catholics to receive the Sacrament of the Holy Eucharist during Easter time, that is, from the first Sunday in Lent to Trinity Sunday.

Ember days: Days of fast and abstinence instituted for the purpose of doing penance and obtaining God's blessing upon the clergy during the season specified for the ceremonies of ordination. The Ember days are: the Wednesdays, Fridays, and Saturdays following the first Sunday of Lent, Pentecost, the feast of the exhaltation of the Cross (September 14), and the third Sunday of Advent.

Ex Cathedra: (Latin) "From the chair," "from the episcopal throne." The pronouncements of the Pope on questions of faith and morals in his official capacity as Teacher of all Christians.

Excommunication: A punishment by which a Christian is deprived of the Sacraments, Christian burial and the prayers of the Church, because of some serious offense which he has committed.

Exegesis: The interpretation of passages of Sacred Scripture.

Exorcism: Prayers and ceremonies used by the Church to drive out devils from persons, places or things.

Fisherman's ring: A ring bearing the figure of St. Peter fishing from a boat and encircled with the name of the pope. This ring is broken upon the Pope's death.

Golden rose: An ornament in the shape of a rose which is blessed by the Pope every year on Laetare Sunday, and sometimes sent by him to Churches, Catholic rulers, or other people of distinction.

Gregorian Mass: Thirty successive Masses said for a deceased person. It is believed that the soul will be released from Purgatory as soon as they are said.

Gregorian Water: Holy Water used in the Consecration of a Church, containing wine, salt, and ashes, and taking its name from Pope Gregory I who prescribed its use.

Grille: An enclosure constructed of wrought iron or bronze, separating the cloister of nuns from the outside.

Heretic: One, who, having been baptized, deliberately and knowingly rejects a doctrine taught by the Catholic Church.

Holy Oils: These are of three kinds: Oil of Catechumens: used in blessing fonts, consecration of churches, ordaining priests, etc. Oil of the sick: used in Extreme Unction. Chrism or oil mixed with balm: used in Baptism, Confirmation, Holy Orders, and other consecrations and blessings.

Holy Orders: A sacrament by which bishops, priests, and other ministers of the Church are ordained and receive the power and grace to perform their sacred duties. There are seven steps by which a cleric advances in succession to the priesthood: Ostiarius (Porter), Exorcist, Lector, Acolyte, Sub-deacon, Deacon, Priest. The first four are called Minor Orders and the last three are called Holy Orders.

Holy Water: A sacramental consisting of water mixed with salt and blessed by a priest; used to bless persons and things.

Immaculate Conception: The doctrine that the creation of Mary's soul, its adornment by sanctifying grace, and its infusion into Mary's body, were all simultaneous. In other words, Mary's soul was never for a moment without sanctifying grace, never for an instant with original sin.

Immersion: Method of Baptism employed in the early Church, by completely immersing the candidate into water. It is still considered as valid Baptism, but it is no longer used in the Western Church.

Imprimatur: Latin word meaning "let it be printed" usually placed at the beginning or end of a publication to indicate that the publication contains nothing against faith and morals and that it has the approval of the bishop.

Imprimi Potest: Latin words meaning "it may be printed" by which the Superior of a religious order approves a publication by a member of the order.

In Petto: From the Italian meaning "in the breast" or "secretly," refers to an occasional decision of the Pope to withhold from publishing the name of a new Cardinal.

Indulgence: A remission granted by the Church of the temporal punishment which remains due to sin, after its guilt has been forgiven. If it remits all punishment it is called plenary. An indulgence may be partial, i. e., part of the temporal punishment of sin is remitted to persons rightly disposed.

Indulgence, Apostolic: Indulgences attached by the Pope or his delegate to crucifixes, rosaries, medals, and other images.

Indult: A permission to do something not allowed by the common law of the Church, such as the Workingman's Indult granted in regard to abstinence.

Infallibility: The inability of the Pope, speaking either alone or together with all the bishops of the Church, to err when he proclaims a teaching of faith or morals.

Jubilee: A period of special remission of the temporal penalties due to sin proclaimed from time to time by the Pope. At present this period occurs every twenty-five years.

Lay brother: A member of a religious order who does not receive holy orders and who does not say the beviary, but who is occupied with the secular affairs of the monastery, as, for example, the care of the buildings, farms, etc.

Legate, papal: An envoy of the Pope sent as his special, personal representative to a sovereign or government or to a special church function to act with the same power as if the Pope himself were present.

Lent: The forty days' fast before Easter, beginning on Ash Wednesday and ending on Holy Saturday at noon.

Martyrology: A list of Martyrs and Saints according to the calendar with brief notices of their life and death, also of the feasts of Our Lord celebrated during the year.

Mass: The unbloody sacrifice of the Body and Blood of Christ made present on the altar by the priest's words of consecration. It is a renewal of the Sacrifice of the Cross.

Mediatrix of All Graces: The blessed Virgin Mary as dispenser of all graces given us by the risen Christ. Some say that Mary intercedes for each and every grace given to us by Christ. Others go further and assert that no grace is given to us unless it first passes through Mary's hands.

Mixed Marriages: Marriage between a Catholic and a validly baptized member of a heretical or schismatic sect or a false religion.

Monk: A member of a religious order, who has the vows of obedience, poverty, and chastity, and who lives according to the rules of his community.

Monsignor: A title given to the members of the Pope's household. The title is sometimes conferred as an honor on priests living outside of Rome.

Motu proprio: (Latin phrase meaning "of one's own accord"): a decree issued by the Pope in his own name without the advice of the cardinals or others.

Movable feasts: Feasts which occur earlier or later in different years, being governed by Easter Sunday, which is always the first Sunday after the first full moon in spring.

Ne Temere: The opening words of a decree issued by Pius X in 1907, stating that thereafter all marriages of Catholics of the Latin Church to be valid, must take place before a qualified parish priest or his delegate and two witnesses.

Nihil Obstat: The words printed in the front part of a book by which the censor of books indicates that he has examined a given work and found nothing in it contrary to faith and morals.

Noble Guard: The highest rank in the Pope's military organization. The Commandment must be a Roman Prince and the members must be of the nobility. A certain number of the Noble Guards always accompany the Pope at a public function.

Novena: Prayers for special graces extending over a period of nine days, in imitation of the Apostles who in prayer awaited the descent of the Holy Ghost.

Nun: A member of a religious order of congregation of women. Nuns, in the strict sense, are those who have solemn vows; Sisters those who have simple vows.

Nuncio: A legate of the Holy See sent as an ambassador to a foreign government as a permanent diplomatic agent.

Pallium: A narrow band woven of white lamb wool granted by the Pope to an Archbishop to be worn on the shoulders over the chasuble. It symbolizes the fullness of episcopal power.

Pastoral letters: Letters addressed by a bishop to the clergy or laity of his diocese.

Patriarch: In the Western Church, the Supreme Pontiff, the Pope. In the Eastern Church, any of the Bishops of the five ancient Sees of Jerusalem, Antioch, Alexandria, Constantinople, Venice.

Pauline privilege: The power of the Catholic Church to dissolve a marriage, even though consummated, of two unbaptized persons—when one is converted to the faith and the other refuses to be converted, or live in peace with the other party; proclaimed by St. Paul.

Pectoral cross: A small cross suspended from the neck and worn on the breast by Bishops and other prelates.

Peter's pence: A voluntary annual contribution made by Catholics to the Holy See.

Plenary Council: A meeting of the Bishops of a region or nation assembled under the presidency of the Pope's legate to determine matters of rule and discipline.

Pope: A word meaning "father," applied to the Bishop of Rome as Vicar of Christ, successor of St. Peter, and head of the Catholic Church.

Relic: The body of a Saint or an integral part of it; also any object that has been sanctified by physical contact with the living saint.

Religious Clergy: Priests organized under a superior of a religious community.

Requiem Mass: A Mass celebrated for a deceased person or persons. Black vestments are always used.

Roman Collar: Collar buttoning in the back to which is attached a silk breast piece called the rabbi, worn by the hierarchy and clergy of the Catholic Church.

Rosary: A devotion in which fifteen decades—each consisting of an Our Father, ten Hail Marys and a Glory be to the Father are recited, and accompanied, each of them, by meditation on one of fifteen mysteries of our Lord, or of our Blessed Lady.

Saint: A person declared by the Church to have cultivated virtue to a heroic degree, to be in heaven and to deserve veneration in the whole Church.

Scapular: A sacramental, a badge of a religious association or order, consisting of two small square woolen pieces connected by two bands, and worn one on the breast and the other on the back. It gives the wearer the right to share in the spiritual blessings of the association or order.

Secular Clergy: Clergy who do not belong to a religious order but labor for the sanctification of souls directly under the authority of the bishop, more properly called diocesan clergy.

Simony: Selling and buying of sacred offices or sacred things.

Solemn Mass: Mass sung by a celebrant with the assistance of a deacon and subdeacon.

Solemn Vows: Vows declared such by the Holy See; a member of a religious community with solemn vows can neither administer nor own property, nor validly contract a marriage without dispensation from his vows.

Stigmata: The five wounds of Our Lord appearing miraculously on the body of any person so favored by God.

Suspension: A penalty by which a cleric is deprived of the exercise of some or all of his powers.

Tiara: The headdress with triple crown worn by the Pope at solemn functions.

Tonsure: A ceremony consisting in cutting off some of the hair from the head, and indicating that the recipient has ceased to be a layman and has been received into the ranks of the clergy. In most Catholic countries the tonsure is made by shaving more or less of the crown of the head.

Toties Quoties: Latin term meaning "as often as." It means that indulgences may be obtained as often as one wishes as long as the necessary conditions are fulfilled, at a specified time or place.

Transubstantiation: The changing of the substance of the bread and wine into the body and blood of Christ at the Consecration of the Mass.

Treasury of the Church: The merits of Christ and the Saints from which the Church draws when she grants indulgences.

Vatican: 160 acres of territory together with the buildings in and about the City of Rome under the rule of the Holy See.

Venial sin: An offense against God which does not destroy the supernatural life of the soul, but weakens the soul, disposing it toward mortal sin.

Viaticum: Holy Communion given to those in probable danger of death. The Latin word "viaticum" means "provision for a journey."

Vulgate: The official Latin version of translation of the Bible used in the Catholic Church. The English Rheims-Douay version is a translation from the Vulgate.—*from* "A CATHOLIC WORD LIST" by Rev. Rudolph C. Bandas

BIBLIOGRAPHY

BALES, JAMES D. *Was Peter Pope?* Berkeley, California.

BAMPFIELD, REV. G. *Mixed Marriages.* Brooklyn, New York, International Catholic Truth Society.

BANDAS, REV. RUDOLPH G. *A Catholic Word List.* Huntington, Indiana, Our Sunday Visitor.

BARONIO, CESARE. *Annales Ecclesiastic.* Vatican Press.

BLANSHARD, PAUL. *American Freedom and Catholic Power.*

Catholic Encyclopedia, The. Volume 12.

Catholic Telegraph. Cincinnati, Ohio, August 25, 1904.

Catholic World, The. New York, 1877.

CHAMBERS, JAMES H. *Errors of the Roman Catholic Church.* St. Louis, Mo.

Churchman Magazine. New York, July, 1949.

CONNELL, FRANCIS J. C.SS. R. *Freedom of Worship, the Catholic Position.* Paulist Press; *The American Ecclesiastic Review.* Washington, D.C., Catholic University, January, 1945.

CREIGHTON, M. A. *A History of the Papacy.* London, Longmans, Green and Company, 1899.

DRAPER, JOHN WILLIAM. *History of the Intellectual Development of Europe.* New York, Harper and Brothers, 1876.

Dublin University Magazine. November, 1845.

FERRARIS' *Ecclesiastical Dictionary,* article on the Pope. Rome, Press of the Propaganda, 1899.

FLICK, ALEXANDER CLARENCE. *The Rise of the Mediaeval Church.* New York, G. P. Putnam's Sons, 1909.

HAGENBACK, DR. K. P. *History of the Reformation in Germany and Switzerland Chiefly.* Edinburgh, T. and T. Clark, 1878.

Harper's Weekly. May 21, 1870.

HUSSEY, ROBERT, B.D. *The Rise of the Papal Power.* Oxford, The Clarendon Press.

JARVIS, JAMES JACKSON. *Italian Rambles,* reproduced by J. H. Eager, D.D. in *Romanism in its Home.* Philadelphia, American Baptist Publication.

LAWRENCE, EUGENE. *Historical Studies.* New York, Harper and Brothers, 1876.

LIGUORI, ST. ALPHONSUS DE. *The Dignity and Duties of the Priests, or Selva.*

MANNING, HENRY EDWARD. *The Temporal Power of the Vicar of Jesus Christ.* London, Burns and Lambert, 1862.

McDONALD, JOHN. *Romanism Analysed*. Edinburgh, Scottish Reform. Society.

MYERS, PHILIP VAN NESS. *Medioeval and Modern History*. Boston, Ginn and Company.

NOLL, BISHOP. *Catholic Facts*. Huntington, Indiana, Our Sunday Visitor.

PARIS, MATTHEY. 1089, 1247.

Quick Magazine. New York, July 11, 1949.

REICHEL, REV. OSWALD J. *The See of Rome in the Middle Ages*. London, Longmans, Green and Company, 1870.

ROBERTSON, JAMES CRAIGIE. *Plain Lectures on the Growth of the Papal Power*. London, Society for Promotion of Christian Knowledge.

Roman Catholic Question Box. New York, Paulist Press.

SCHULTE, PAUL C. *Fatima and You*. Huntington, Indiana, Our Sunday Visitor.

Source Book for Bible Students. Washington, D.C., Review and Herald Publishing Association, 1922.

TAYLOR, JEREMY. *Of the Marriage of Bishops and Priests*.

VON DOLLINGER, DR. J. J. IGN. *The Church and Churches*. London, Hurst and Blackett. *The Pope and the Council*. London, Rivingston. 1869.

WOOD, LELAND FOSTER. *If I Marry a Catholic*. New York.

INDEX

Excerpts from the Sword Book Club Judges Reviews of

SECRETS OF ROMANISM

by JOSEPH ZACCHELLO

Dr. V. Raymond Edman, President, Wheaton College, Wheaton, Illinois.
"A thoughtful, careful, well documented statement of the unscriptural basis of the Roman Catholic faith. The author states his thesis succinctly in the opening statement of the Introduction—'The best book against Romanism was not written by a Protestant or by a former priest, but by God. It is the BIBLE.' . . . The treatment is remarkably free from malice and vindictiveness, and is very enlightening to both Protestants and Catholics."

Dr. T. Roland Philips, Pastor, Arlington Presbyterian Church, Baltimore.
"The title of this book reveals its contents. It was written by one who should know the subject, for he was trained in a Roman seminary in Italy and served as a Roman priest in various cities in the United States. . . . This book will enlighten any who may not know what Roman Catholics are taught, and it will help those who are seeking to help Catholics know the truth."

Evangelist William Rice, Wheaton, Illinois.
"I am not sure whether this book will be more beneficial to Catholics or to Protestants, but both definitely should read it. Many Catholics do not know why they believe what they believe, do not know on what foundation their creeds and doctrines are based, and do not realize the extent of their deception. On the other hand, many Protestants do not really know what Catholicism teaches nor why so much of it is error. . . . This is a book well worth having."

Dr. Robert G. Lee, Pastor, Bellevue Baptist Church, Memphis, Tenn.
". . . Using the Roman version of the Bible as his authority, the author proves that each doctrine taught by the Catholic church is false, and even contrary to the teachings of the Roman Bible. In other words, the Roman Bible itself condemns Romanism. . . . It gives the answers to many questions that have arisen, not only in the Christian's mind, who would like to help his struggling Catholic friend, but to the Catholics themselves who are blind to the true teachings of the Bible."

Dr. Bob Jones, Jr., President, Bob Jones University, Greenville, S. C.
"This book is a better than average expose of Roman Catholicism. It is free from the sensationalism usually found in such a book. . . . "

Dr. Henry Hepburn, Pastor Emeritus, Buena Memorial Presbyterian Church, Chicago.
"An amazing volume. One that fills a present day need, for here is an authoritative clear cut picture of the Roman Church. Many questions of the history and practices of the Church are clearly revealed. This book should be in the hands of Christians to help them meet the problems and questions that arise relative to the Roman Church. . . ."